Talking to Children about Sex

Talking
to Children
about Sex

EDNA S. LEHMAN

HAR/ROW BOOKS

Harper & Row, Publishers
New York

First HAR/ROW BOOK edition published 1970

Library of Congress Catalog Card Number: 72-85063

To the hundreds of children
it has been my privilege to know

Preface

"Sex education belongs in the home." "Sex education must be taught in our schools." These two familiar statements are the basis of many a lively conversation. And in many of them, the child has been forgotten.

The parent who insists it is his right to teach his child about sex is correct. Does he accept the challenge he has given himself? Is he prepared to teach his child and guide him? Is he doing a good job in the light of today's world?

Educators who insist the schools must accept the challenge of teaching our children about themselves and their sex are also correct. Schools have discovered that only a small proportion of our youth are knowledgeable about sex and have received their instruction in the home. The majority of children have gathered their information (mostly misinformation) from their peers.

The high incidence of syphilis among teen-agers (which is growing larger every year), the startling number of unwed teen-age mothers, the young people who are indulging in sexual intercourse for a lark, are not bringing happiness and dignity to themselves or others. The author feels that family living and sex education should be taught in the home, and supplemental teaching should take place in the school classroom. Thus working together, all children will be reached.

It has been the author's privilege to teach in the Evanston Elementary Schools, where sex education was pioneered many years ago. In the beginning, the fifth-grade level was selected at which to teach the child about himself. Parents were invited each year to a meeting, at which time they were informed of the program. Their acceptance and enthusiasm and suggestions were an invaluable aid in the improvement of the curriculum.

Within the last five years, the program has been extended to include all children from kindergarten through eighth grade, with the goal in mind of helping all children to see the wonder of nature: the way all living things are reproduced, the manner in which each living thing in some way benefits other living things, the balance of nature, the importance of all living things to human beings, and most important of all, the miracle of human birth and growth. A curriculum has been prepared for all grade levels (in which the author has been actively involved), and the teachers attend an In-Service workshop to prepare them for teaching this important subject.

The purpose of this book is to help parents and teachers fulfill their responsibilities and achieve their purpose of aiding our boys and girls in learning about God's blueprint of life. The author is sharing some of her experiences and thoughts in this book, hopeful that it will serve to help readers reach their goal. This will be her richest reward.

Contents

PREFACE   vii

CHAPTER ONE   1
The Baby
The new infant. The toddler. Answering the toddler's questions. Correct vocabulary. Toilet training. The toddler learns that there are males and females.

CHAPTER TWO   9
The Three-Year-Old
Abilities and behavior. Three's world expands. Sex understanding at three. The innocence of three. Discovering friends. Imaginary playmates. Parents. The new baby. The displaced baby. Learning about breasts. Avoiding jealousy.

CHAPTER THREE   23
Age Four
On being four. The curious four-year-old. Group play. Dramatic play. Stress reactions. Noise. Listening. Teaching modesty. Questions about babies. Misconceptions about birth. Today's child and birth information. Religion and sex education.

CHAPTER FOUR   37
Age Five
The five-year-old child. Playmates. Reactions to tension. Being boys and girls. "Crushes" and fan-

tasies. Masturbation. The new baby. Questions
about babies. Sex play. Kindergarten—unit on
family. Kindergarten—new babies. Kindergarten—
animal babies. Kindergarten—sex pictures. Kindergarten—parent cooperation.

CHAPTER FIVE   59
   Age Six
The six-year-old child. Sex differences. Learning
respect for privacy. Correct vocabulary. The first
grade learns about the family. Learning about
animal babies.

CHAPTER SIX   75
   The Seven-Year-Old at Home
The seven-year-old child. Gross bodily outlets.
Seven's fears. Child-family relations. The seven-
year-old child's socializing. The seven-year-old and
sex. The father and mother roles. Animal reproduction. A dog in the family.

CHAPTER SEVEN   91
   The Seven-Year-Old at School
Behavior at school. Plant reproduction. The
school teaches animal reproduction. Amphibious
animals. Fish. More egg-laying animals. Mammals
reproduce. Extinct animals. The importance of an
egg. Human beings. When babies grow. Answering
questions.

CHAPTER EIGHT   123
   The Eight-Year-Old at Home and School
Behavior at eight. Peer groups. The eight-year-old
and sex. Masturbation. Boys and the new baby.
Children's questions. At school. Learning about
family patterns. Science. Human beings reproduce.

CHAPTER NINE   145
   The Nine-Year-Old at Home
Behavior at nine. The child and family. Peer
groups. Outlets for tension. Nine and sex. Need

for guidance. Boys should be boys. Girls should
be girls. Listen, learn, and guide.

CHAPTER TEN   167
  The Nine-Year-Old at School
  Behavior at school. Learning about the family.
  Life begins with life. Learning about plant cells.
  Chromosomes and genes. Seeing living cells and
  blood circulation. More cells. Reproduction cells.
  Protozoa. Other living animals.

CHAPTER ELEVEN   179
  The Preadolescent at Home
  Behavior characteristics. Behavior at ten. Ten and
  sex. Behavior at eleven. Eleven and sex. Behavior
  at twelve. Twelve and sex. Parents' behavior. Puzzled parents. Forming attitudes toward sex. Home
  and school encourage learning. Questions asked of
  parents. Timetables.

CHAPTER TWELVE   205
  The Preadolescent at School
  Behavior at school. Preadolescent needs. Body
  systems. Cells and body growth. Fertilization of
  ova. The fetus. The baby is born. Unwed mothers.
  Boy or girl? Multiple births. Separating the sexes.
  Teaching aids. Parent involvement. Sixth- and
  seventh-grade children.

GLOSSARY   235

BIBLIOGRAPHY   239

Chapter One

The Baby

The new infant

Sex education starts the first time you hold your new-born baby. The loving arms, the gentle caressing, the adoring voices all give this miracle of life a feeling of security and love.

Feeding time is a comforting and pleasurable experience for baby as he rests his head on mother's soft breast and sucks in the warm nourishment that comes from breast or bottle.

Bath time brings its rewards to the infant, too. How good to feel mother's gentle stroking as she lovingly washes face, arms, body, and genital area and then cuddles him warmly in the large, soft towel!

The infant soon learns that having his diaper changed also brings pleasant feelings to him. The loving voice of his parent, the gentle stroking and patting that accompany diaper changing soon make it one of the nice times of the day for him. But if he hears unpleasant sounds and sees disagreeable faces being made by an adult who finds changing a soiled diaper a revolting task, he will soon learn that something is wrong and bad about the whole process.

As the baby grows he learns not only about mother

and father and the things they do for him, but about himself, too. At about six weeks he begins to see clearly and discovers his hands for the first time, and examines them critically. His hands, he soon finds, are good for feeling things. They examine crib, blankets, face, and those delightful toes. One day those hands discover his genital organs. How good this feels to him. It is only natural that he touch them, for he has no preconceived ideas about what to touch and what not to touch. The wise parent ignores his exploring.

The toddler

As the baby grows and becomes a toddler, he is experimenting and learning constantly. Parents' attitudes are quickly caught by the little one at this time. For example, a two-year-old boy is handling and pulling at his pants in the penis area while he is watching mother busy at the stove preparing his lunch.

MOTHER: *Don't do that, it's naughty!*
CHILD: Why?
MOTHER: *We don't touch ourselves there!*

The toddler has learned that the penis area must be bad. If ignored, he would most likely stop the handling soon. If the touching and pulling is excessive, it might be well later to make sure that his pants are comfortable and not too tight or binding. For the moment, mother could divert his attention with, "Will you open the cupboard door and get the little pan for me?"

The child of one or two has so much to learn that he seems to be into everything; wastebaskets get turned upside down and the contents distributed, oranges are rolled on the floor, pots and pans must be watched or they will all be taken out of the cupboard, shoes or toys may be thrown into the toilet. The wise parent knows that the toddler is not being naughty or trying to exasperate his family. This is part of a normal baby's way of learning.

Answering the toddler's questions

When the baby points with delight at a moving train, the parent may say, "That's a train. See how fast it goes! It's taking lots of people for a ride. Someday we'll take you for a ride on the train."

Similar answers are eagerly given by parents if the child asks about mother's ears or father's hairy legs; but let him ask about mother's breast or father's penis and many parents freeze, not knowing what to say. The toddler expects an answer, which he may remember or forget. How can these questions be answered?

TOMMY: *What's that (pointing to mother's breast)?*
MOTHER: *These are my breasts. Women are made to be mothers, and they all have breasts. When I have a little baby, there will be milk in my breasts to feed the tiny baby.*
TOMMY: *Tommy drank milk when he was a baby.*
MOTHER: *Yes, and you liked it.*
TOMMY: *Tommy want some now.*
MOTHER: *There is no milk there now. When babies grow big like you, they can drink milk from a cup. My breasts don't need to have milk anymore.*

Your child may not want to know this much about a woman's breasts or anything else he asks about. It is a good rule to answer only the question; but be sure you do answer it, and with the same natural tone and manner as you used when you talked about the train.

He may ask the same question over and over, but this is necessary for him because he forgets easily. Answering questions patiently and in good humor helps your child learn and encourages him to come to you for information.

Correct vocabulary

It is at this age of one or two that a child will see
mother or father dressing or undressing, for he is near
one parent or the other most of his waking hours. This
is a good age for him to see the male and female nude
bodies. It is the time to start using the correct names
for all body parts and functions. The toddler often gives
them pet names, typical of his age, but parents should
continue to use the correct terminology, though per-
mitting the baby to enjoy his made-up vocabulary. All
little children are curious about their navel. Use the
correct name rather than "belly button." Family pet
names for parts of the body often prove embarrassing
to the child when he is away from home.

In a primary classroom a child referred to a part of
the body using the term "belly button," and immediately the children broke into laughter and silly
giggles. The teacher brought the class back to their
serious discussion by saying, "I'm glad you mentioned
the navel. Every human being has a navel, and it serves
a very important part in our being alive." Needless to
say, the little girl used the correct term after that.

Using such words as urinate, bowel movement, or
toilet with your youngster gives dignity to the function
and is understood by all, rather than family pet or slang
words such as "wee-wee," "tinkle," "grunt," or "bum-
bum." Doctors have found that many young adults avoid
going for medical help because they do not know the
correct names of body parts needed to explain their
ailment. They are embarrassed to use the baby or vulgar
words they were taught at home or in the alley.

The toddler should hear words such as breasts, penis,
urinate, bowel movement, uterus, vulva, vagina, testicle,
anus, and pregnant. As he grows older, additional

vocabulary will be added, giving the child the language he will need in his discussions with parents, doctors, or in the classroom.

The little child just learning to say words often experiments with them and repeats them over and over. The word "No" is one the toddler particularly enjoys. He has just discovered that it brings a reaction from others which he has not experienced before, so he may "No" everything that happens for several days. He may choose other words to practice, such as "urinate," which the parent finds irritating. Biting the lip and ignoring the chant usually proves to be the best remedy. If the parent cannot tolerate hearing the child practice such words, a substitute word or words can be suggested. The adult may say, "You've practiced that word long enough. Now try these fun words, 'silly-dilly.' These words rhyme. Can you say 'silly-dilly'?"

Toilet training

Another area of learning that often causes problems to the little child and his parents is toilet training. It is most important that a child should not get the notion that the organs of elimination are dirty or bad, for later in life, due to their proximity, this attitude may be transferred to the reproductive organs. Parents can help the child learn that every part of his body is wonderfully made, and each organ has a very special function to perform. Life itself is dependent on the elimination of waste products!

Mothers are often anxious to have their child toilet trained, but they must remember that impatient training is self-defeating.

Most children are not ready for bowel control until their second year of life, or urinary control until their third year. Naturally there are exceptions, but do not strive too hard to make your child the exception. Remember also that children will have accidents up to age five.

Toddlers often have bowel movements about the same time each day. When a mother feels that her baby is ready to try for bowel control, she should start at the child's natural time for elimination. A small toilet or baby seat that fits on the regular toilet seat should be introduced to the toddler.

MOTHER: *See, here is a toilet seat for you. Now you can use the toilet the way mother and father do. Here, let me help you.*
TODDLER: *Tommy big!*
MOTHER: *Yes, you are getting bigger.*

Mother's smiles and encouragement can make this a pleasant experience for the baby. If it is unsuccessful, show no disappointment but encourage your child by saying, "You sat so well on your new toilet seat. Next time perhaps you'll have a bowel movement when you are on the toilet seat."

If the child is successful, a word of praise is reward enough. Care should be taken not to expect the baby to sit on the seat for too long a time, or he will learn to dread the sessions.

Urinary control can be approached in the same manner. Many children urinate immediately on awakening in the morning or after a nap. Again, the mother can start the training at the times she has noted are fairly regular elimination times. Simple training pants are helpful at this time. Diapers or complicated overalls often cause accidents, when the child cannot wait until he is free of them, or may cause him to resent the time taken for such an uninteresting activity. Success cannot be attained with such hurdles.

The adult's good humor and patience make it easier for a child to train himself. He should feel neither guilt nor defeat when he has an "accident." Some children will announce to the adult: "Wet!" if his bed is wet in the morning. A parent may say in a friendly voice, "Yes, the bed is wet. Too bad!" This will not draw the attention to the child, but rather to the wet sheet. The child also knows it would be better if the bed were dry.

Elimination control is a desirable and necessary goal for the small child. A patient, consistent, organized mother is a necessary part of this training. How can a child achieve success, if mother cannot remember to be his dependable helper?

Occasionally a small child will play with or feel the body product after his bowel movements. This is not unusual and does not mean that your child has anything wrong with him. It does mean that he looks upon it in the same way that he does all other things about him. Your horrified, "Don't do that, it's dirty!" is harmful. Naturally you will not want him to do this. Calmly flush the toilet, wash his hands, and give him a substitute. Water play or modeling clay are two delightful substitutes for the toddler.

The toddler learns that there are males and females

In a home where parents allow the toddler to see their nude bodies and those of his brothers and sisters, he will learn naturally and gradually that there are males and females. An only child must have the experience of seeing nude children near his own age, also. Parents should plan for this as carefully as they plan trips to the zoo or to the airport to see the planes. The toddler could be taken to see a new baby, and see it fed, bathed, and diapered. The same and the opposite sex should be viewed. It is reassuring to a child to see that there are other children just like himself. This is a good time to learn that there is an opposite sex, also. A little girl watching a baby boy have his bath showed a great interest in the whole procedure. The baby's mother talked to her about the care she took to keep soap out of the baby's eyes, and demonstrated how tiny and helpless the baby was.

MARY: (Pointing to baby's penis.) *Look! What's that?*
ADULT: *That's his penis. He's a boy baby. All boys have a penis.*
MARY: *Mary will get a penis.*
ADULT: *No, only boys have a penis. You're a girl. You have a uterus. All girls and ladies have a uterus.*
MARY: *What's a uterus?*
ADULT: *It's a special place in girls and women. When you're grown up and married and want a baby, the baby will grow in the uterus.*
MARY: *Show Mary.*
ADULT: *No, your uterus is inside you and you can't see it. But it's there.*

If the child does not ask questions, the parent should point out the difference and start the discussions.

Sometimes a little boy will grow concerned when he discovers that the baby girl is different. He fears that she has lost her penis and that he might lose his, too. He needs to be reassured as to losing his penis and to be told that the girl does not have one because she is a girl. Toddlers should be permitted to view each other in the bathroom. It is a good age to learn that the process of urination is different for boys and girls.

By the time the baby has reached the age of three, he has learned much: he has discovered that some things bring pleasure and give him a lovely warm feeling, while some bring bad feelings and make him miserable. At this early age, he has learned the difference.

Chapter Two

The Three-Year-Old

Abilities and behavior

The three-year-old is beginning to leave the infant behavior of one and two behind and is becoming more of a little child. He can use crayons, enjoys a simple jigsaw puzzle, runs more surely and easily, rides a tricycle, and learns to handle a spoon and cup so well that spilling is greatly reduced. He can unbutton front buttons, pull up a simple zipper, and untie shoelaces.

It can be frustrating for a mother that her three-year-old enjoys untying his shoelaces and taking the laces completely out of the shoes, but what a victory for him! Mother can take comfort in his desire to learn and his interest in dressing and undressing himself. Before too many months pass, the little one will become quite proficient and will only need help with the hard parts, such as buttons that are difficult to reach, and tying shoelaces.

The impatient mother who finds it easier quickly to dress the three-year-old, rather than let him clumsily fumble with his own clothing and end up with his sweater inside out, is cheating her child of an important learning-readiness experience. Small wonder that some five- or even six-year-old children arrive at school unable to tie their own shoes or put on boots and heavy coats.

They seem to have lost the impulse to try to learn and want parent and teacher to wait on them.

By three, the child is usually toilet-trained, except for those accidents which do occur from time to time. He wants to bathe himself and tries to prolong his bath by insisting that he needs to do more scrubbing or rinsing.

Pleasing an adult is usually important to the three-year-old. He often makes statements about himself such as, "Jimmy is a good boy," as though trying to convince himself that he is pleasing to others. In his desire to be agreeable, he enjoys following simple directions. "Put the toy truck on the bottom shelf!" is a challenge to him and provides a way he can prove to adults and himself that he is getting bigger. With a bit of parent participation and encouragement, putting toys away or socks in a drawer is almost as much fun as taking them out. It is also teaching him to follow directions, a most necessary part of learning.

Many children at this age will undress a doll when presented with one, and will contentedly play with a nude doll. Some parents will be concerned about this and fear that their child has wrong inclinations, since removing the doll's clothes seems so important. The truth of the matter is that most children of this age enjoy the challenge of removing the doll's clothes, but find dressing it beyond their ability.

Three's world expands

At about this age, a child begins to discover that the world outside the home is exciting, and he wants to be a part of it. Susan, who lives down the block, has a tricycle, and it is nice for Michael to ride on the sidewalk next to her. Jimmy has a sandbox, and it is more fun when two are in the box scooping up sand and digging holes. Sometimes three-year-old friends laugh together, sometimes tears roll when they both want the same shovel; most of the time each child is consumed with his own activity, but finds it more enjoyable if a friend is near by.

A child this age still does not know how to share, and he is still self-centered, but he is learning that other children are nice to be near. He permits another child to use his tricycle, if he doesn't want it himself at that particular moment. He seems to flit from one thing to another, yet can become maddeningly persistent about an occasional activity.

Three-year-old Michael discovered a beautiful puddle made by his neighbor's lawn hose in a sunken part of the sidewalk. He had just come from a bath and was gleaming in fresh clothes and combed hair, but that water was so inviting in the ninety-degree heat! He experimented by walking through the puddle. That was fun, and his toes liked the squishy feeling inside his shoes. Soon he was stomping through the puddle, splashing water in all directions. Michael looked at his parents. They didn't say a thing (it happened that their backs were turned, talking to a neighbor).

Heartened by their silence, Michael began vigorously to enjoy the puddle, kicking the water with great glee. He slipped and fell with a splash. Then the water became a real challenge! He rolled in it, he washed his hair in the now muddy water, he even tasted it.

At this moment the father noticed his water-soaked son. Calmly he walked over and said firmly, "Water is fun, I know, but you are not to play in it when you are in clean clothes. Now, back to the bathtub with you, and next time ask to have your swim trunks put on." With that, he picked up his dripping son and carried him at arm's length into the house.

Michael learned that what he had done was not pleasing to his parent, but he also knew that he had an understanding father. How much better this is than anger, slaps, insults, and a rebellious youngster. Too often we hear "What's the matter with you?" "Are you crazy?" "How can you do such a bad thing to your mother?" "You'll be the death of her yet!" "All she does is work and work to keep you clean." "You're a bad, bad boy! Now get in the house!" "There won't be any stories for you tonight."

A child who hears such anger and accusations from a quick-tempered father often gains a poor opinion of himself, and perhaps even develops feelings of guilt about killing his mother. In the mind of a child such a father may also appear a tyrant—someone to fear and dislike. Here Michael has not only learned that his father is understanding and wants his son to have good behavior, but he is also gaining a good father image to emulate when he becomes an adult. This father is taking his rightful place in the family by being both a loving teacher and a firm authority to his child.

Sex understanding at three

Three-year-old children have a fairly clear idea that there are mommies and daddies, boys and girls, brothers and sisters, men and women, grandmothers and grandfathers. Some children have learned that there are "boy dogs" and "girl dogs" and "mama dogs." Little by little their experiences are teaching them that there are two sexes and many kinds of people. Some of these people are special to the child and some just go by on the sidewalks or in cars. He has learned by this age that once he was a little baby, but now he is growing bigger and is not a little baby anymore.

A child this age does not always function as a male or female. They seem to vacillate from one sex role to another. Little Nancy tries to play football with her big brother. The next minute she will be the mama when she and Michael play with the doll and buggy. Sometimes Michael gets tired of being the daddy and switches to being the mommy. At three this is normal play.

Parents can help Michael learn that he is a boy by helping him learn his role in the family. Nancy, too, is helped by a mother and father who treat her as a little girl, letting her know that they are glad she is a girl and that being a girl is very nice. In the same way, Michael learns that his family is happy that he is a boy, and he is treated like a boy.

The innocence of three

The three-year-old is honest and innocent, unless he has learned from older people that some things are bad. This age announces in front of company, "I have to go to the toilet." He is very apt to pop nude into an afternoon tea his mother is having, to announce that he cannot find his underwear. One mother was shocked to see her small son and the neighbor's little girl come unconcernedly up the front walk completely nude, carrying their clothes crumpled into a ball in their arms. Controlling herself, she asked why they had taken their clothes off.

"We ran through the sprinkler. We took off our clothes so they wouldn't get wet," was the practical answer. The mother asked them to put their clothes back on and then said matter-of-factly, "When people are out of doors, they keep their clothes on. If you want to play in water, you are to put on your swim suits."

Anger or laughter directed at the two nudists would have affected their attitudes about nudity in an unwholesome way. As it was handled by the mother, they felt neither guilty nor foolish, but did hear once more about proper attire out of doors.

Little girls at this age often find fascinating the posture little boys assume when urinating, and they will also try to urinate standing in front of the toilet. Naturally they meet with little or no success; parents' patience is needed, for small children have much to learn by the trial-and-error method.

Timmy was given a dog for his birthday, and he carefully studied the dog's every move. He tried eating his food the way his dog did, but discovered it was pretty messy. "Your mouth is different from a dog's," his mother pointed out calmly.

When Timmy's father came home from work, he was embarrassed to see his little boy trying to urinate against a tree the way the new dog did. The father hustled his son into the house and was ready to apply a strong hand, when his wife pointed out that Timmy had been pretending all day that he was a dog. Then Timmy, mother, and father calmly talked about appropriate dog behavior and child behavior. Timmy understood, and from his own experimenting had learned that there was a difference. He turned his attention to other things and the dog episodes were over.

Discovering friends

At about three and a half years of age, children often form deep though temporary attachments for one special playmate. Parents must often be firm about separating them for lunch or afternoon naps, for they beg to spend every waking hour together. At this age they do not seem to notice the sex of their playmate; a little girl will choose her own or the opposite sex for her companion, and their games and ways of playing will be similar.

Some parents, fathers particularly, often tease a little boy for cuddling a doll or pushing a doll carriage. Perhaps the child is merely imitating his own father, who certainly enjoys his babies. Many a little boy enjoys pushing a doll carriage, especially when the girl with whom he is playing wants to play "mommy and daddy."

If a father finds it irritating to see his son enjoying feminine toys, he can substitute a toy shopping cart or wagon. It is the enjoyment of pushing or pulling possessions about that has the great appeal for the child. Also a Teddy bear or stuffed dog is just as satisfying to cuddle as a doll.

It is not surprising that three-year-old children like to play mommy and daddy, for this is something they know well and admire. Also, at this age they advance to understanding that there are husbands and wives and that they are married. They hear and learn that men and women get married and have babies.

The three-year-old often proposes marriage to father or mother or to anyone else for whom he has gained an attachment. The phrases "I love" and "Do you love me?" become a much-used part of his vocabulary, particulary if he is a member of a family that uses these affectionate expressions.

Imaginary playmates

Age three will also often have imaginary playmates. Little Carol had Trixie and Traycondatz as her companions. If Carol had a tumble, she would blame Trixie for pushing her. It seemed more satisfying to blame the imaginary. Trixie than to admit her own clumsiness in falling. When Carol was given a cookie she often asked for extras for Traycondatz and Trixie. Her parents were never able to determine whether these two pretend creatures were animals or human beings, for Carol herself did not seem sure of their identity. But friends they were, who frequently became a part of her solitary play, and her father often had to let them sit next to him during story time. After two years of inhabiting Carol's home, she announced one day that they had moved, and to this day Trixie and Traycondatz have never returned.

Parents

The three-year-old child often finds mother his favorite person. It is she who usually spends her days with him, feeding him, comforting him when unhappiness strikes, teaching him new things, taking him to the stores, and setting limits for him. Mother is the all-wise, all-loving authority in his life.

If father spends most of his leisure time with his family, then he is often the three-year-old's next favorite person. Father is the strong and intelligent person who brings new experiences to the small child; he can carry children on his shoulders, he mows the lawn and puts on the storm windows, he takes the family on a vacation, he likes to tuck the little ones into their beds and is the final answer about many things affecting the family.

It usually proves best for Junior if his father has authority over certain affairs and the mother over her specialties. It is important that parents agree on discipline and authority. In the household where parents both have authority for each activity and rule, the child will soon learn to play one parent against the other, to the detriment of his own security and personality.

Susan's parents had never given much thought to discipline and authority and the part each of them played in the life of their child, yet they were angry and disappointed when she learned undesirable methods of getting her own way.

SUSAN: *Mommy, I'm going to Liz's house now.*
MOTHER: *No, Susan, it's nearly time for your bath.*
SUSAN: *I want to go. I don't want a bath. Please, Mommy, please!*
MOTHER: *No, Susan, you're to stay at home. You may go to Liz's house tomorrow.*

Susan looked at her mother and studied her face. She knew her mother was firm about decisions.

She went in search of her father. He was far enough away not to have heard her mother tell Susan to stay indoors. So Susan decided to see if she could get his permission.

SUSAN: *Daddy, I want to go out and play with Liz.*
FATHER: *Where will you play?*
SUSAN: *At Liz's house. She wants me. Please, Daddy?*
FATHER: *It isn't dinnertime yet. I guess it's all right.*

How much better it would have been if her father had told Susan, "Mother is the one to ask about that, for she knows your play times."

The new baby

Just as a child this age learns about marriage and fathers and mothers, he also discovers that mommies and daddies have babies. "Can we have a new baby" is often asked by the three-year-old child. He is sure it would be wonderful having a new baby in his very own home. When the baby does arrive, he may be completely disillusioned; the new baby is not a playmate. It sleeps most of the time. It cries a lot and takes much too much of his mother's time.

Parents who prepare the young children in the family for the new baby's arrival can do much to alleviate the disenchantment and jealousy that may arise. When they are helped to understand before the baby arrives that it will be a helpless little human being whose very existence depends on his family, it will not be too shocking to find this new family member joining them with no abilities other than sleeping, sucking, crying, and soiling diapers.

Parents should grasp every opportunity to prepare the child for the baby. When the child refers to the baby's arrival, discuss it with him.

CHILD: When the baby comes, I'll give him a ride on my tricycle.

PARENT: The baby won't be able to ride on your tricycle. All it can do is sleep and cry and drink milk.

CHILD: Why?

PARENT: Because it will be a baby just born, and it isn't strong enough even to sit up. When the baby grows as big and old as you, it can ride your tricycle.

CHILD: I couldn't ride a tricycle when I was a baby.

PARENT: That's right. You had to grow strong enough and big enough to sit on your tricycle and pedal. That takes a long, long time.

CHILD: I was a little baby when you got me. That was a long time ago.

PARENT: Once you were a tiny baby. Now you're big enough to help me take care of our new tiny baby when it's born.

The three-year-old child will ask, even though he has heard it before, where the baby will come from.

CHILD: Why don't we get the baby today?

MOTHER: It's not time yet for it to be born. We have to wait for many days.

CHILD: Where will we get our baby?

MOTHER: It's growing in a special baby-growing place in my body.

CHILD: Show me.

MOTHER: We can't see the baby yet, but I can feel it moving inside my uterus.

If the child is curious, the mother can suggest that he put his hands on her abdomen to see how round it is getting with the baby growing inside her uterus. If movement can be felt, the child can feel it and may be told the baby is moving its hands or feet.

Many children at this age cannot comprehend that the new baby actually grew in the mother's body. Some three-year-old children repeat what they have been told and convince their parents that they have done a good job of teaching, only to shatter the parents' smugness by asking, on the baby's arrival, if the doctor gave them the baby. But the teaching has not been in vain, for certain facts remain in the child's mind to be added to from time to time as he grows older.

The displaced baby

The new baby is not automatically loved by the youngest child who has been the family baby. The new baby has changed his position in the family, and that in itself can prove to be a nagging problem. Mother and father and other relatives and friends spend a good deal of time admiring and studying that new bundle of life. It can be threatening to the displaced baby to see so much attention heaped on the new one.

Parents can help the little child overcome his doubts and fears concerning the new baby. He may need extra physical love at this time, as in sitting on his mother's lap for a bit of fondling. Baby's schedule should not interfere with the small child's meals or special little times with mother or father.

Three-year-old Martha was asked by her mother to watch the new baby get a bath and was allowed gently to stroke some soap on the baby's feet. It helped Martha feel she was a part of the baby's life. Occasionally, getting a clean diaper for the baby or handing her mother the can of powder made her feel important and capable. While the baby was nursing, Martha's mother often had quiet conversations with her. It was also a good time to help Martha become acquainted with her new brother.

MOTHER: *See the baby's tiny fingers? They look so little next to yours.*
MARTHA: *Look at my big hand!*
MOTHER: *Your hand is much larger and you can do many things with your hands.*
MARTHA: *Baby can't do things with his hands, can he?*

MOTHER: You're right. He can't do the things you can do. He can hold on to things, though. That's one thing his hands can do. Put your finger gently up to his hand and see what happens.

MARTHA: He's holding my finger. He likes me, see!

MOTHER: Yes, baby likes you. You're so gentle with him, and that makes him happy.

Learning about breasts

The three-year-old is very interested in nursing, and asks many questions.

MARTHA: Why does the baby get dinner from you?

MOTHER: Baby hasn't any teeth. He can't eat food the way you do. He has to drink milk.

MARTHA: Why doesn't he drink milk out of a cup, like I do?

MOTHER: He's too little to teach. All he can do is suck. He can suck the milk from my breast.

MARTHA: How do you get the milk in there?

MOTHER: When a mother has a baby, milk develops in the mother's breasts.

MARTHA: Do all mommies have milk in their breasts?

MOTHER: Only mothers who have new babies.

MARTHA: Can I have some?

MOTHER: The milk is for new babies. You won't like it now that you're big. You can taste it if you want to.

Most children, after one taste of the warm milk, announce that they are glad their milk comes from the refrigerator.

Often the small child will inspect himself to see if he has breasts. Little boys are often overjoyed to see that they have the beginnings of breasts. They will announce to their mother that they have breasts and will feed their baby when they grow up.

MOTHER: You have breasts, Billy, but you won't have milk in them. You'll be a father, and fathers don't nurse babies. Only mothers who have new babies have milk in their breasts.

BILLY: But look, Mommy, I have breasts right here!

MOTHER: Yes, Billy, everyone has breasts just as everyone has eyes and ears, but only mothers have milk grow in them. You'll grow up to be a father. You'll work and earn money so you can have a good home for your baby, just the way your daddy does.

Avoiding jealousy

There are times when the baby completely disregards the family's rights and demands attention. If it doesn't happen too often, children can be helped to accept the interruptions, even though they are annoying.

MOTHER: The baby's crying again, and here we are, right in the middle of our story.

MARTHA: I don't want you to go! Keep reading, Mommy.

MOTHER: That is what I'd like to do. You and I want to enjoy our story. It's hard to stop, but something is bothering our baby. If you stay right here, I'll check the baby and then come right back to finish the story with you. You hold the book.

MARTHA: Tell that baby to stop crying.

Letting the child know that his disappointment is understood helps him to accept it more easily. If possible, the mother should return to the three-year-old and the story should continue as quickly as possible. There are times, however, when she cannot return immediately, so may confide in the young child as Martha's mother did.

MOTHER: Martha, please come here; I want to talk to you.

MARTHA: Here's my book. Will you read now?

MOTHER: Look at our baby. She spit up, and I have to wash her and clean her bed, I need someone to help me. Will you help me?

MARTHA: I'll help, Mommy.

MOTHER: Good. I'll wrap a clean blanket around baby and put her on my big bed. You watch her carefully, while I change the sheets on her bed.

When calm is restored, the mother should thank her young daughter and go back to the story. It will also help Martha to feel more important if the mother tells the father on his return from work how helpful Martha has been to her and the new baby.

Involving the child as often as possible will keep good rapport among mother, child, and baby. Being ignored or pushed aside causes the small child to feel neglected. He soon feels that his parents' love has been transferred to the new baby, and this in turn causes jealousy and hate toward the intruder.

Little children have so much to learn during the first few years of life, it is not surprising that they make many errors along the way. Parents must exercise patience, good humor, and wisdom, for they are the guides, encouragers, and safe haven for these new, eager little learners. It is from their parents that they are learning what is good and what is bad. Their adjustment to life is being molded by their experiences and their family's reaction to them.

Chapter Three

Age Four

On being four

Curiosity, talkativeness, boasting, boundless energy, and constant activity, all are part of the four-year-old child's make-up.

He seems to enjoy hearing his own voice and words, and has discovered the word *I*. He no longer uses his name when referring to himself, but seems to use the personal pronoun in every sentence he utters: "I don't want to." "I know how to do it." "I tell you to do it."

Age four often asks "Why?" without waiting to hear the answer. He is bossy and refuses ever to be wrong, yet is quick to criticize others and may say, "He's dumb. He does dumb things." He enjoys telling about things that happen to him and often embellishes the stories with a brazen air of innocence. He talks so much, and with such assertiveness, that he is often judged to be much more knowledgeable than he really is.

Mother is still the lodestar of his existence. He relies on her to comfort him when he is afraid, and he may have many unreasonable fears that seem to have no foundation. Mother takes care of him when he is sick and cuddles him when he feels unhappy. She feeds him and knows all the answers to his endless questions.

The four-year-old child is developing great pride in his

family and has a strong feeling of loyalty to each member. "My mommy says so" is his most convincing argument with outsiders. "My daddy knows everything" really takes care of all contenders in his mind.

There are some children who are apt to reject their fathers at this age if they feel that he comes between them and their mother, or if he neglects and ignores them. Fortunately, most four-year-old children love their father and especially prize short excursions or times alone with him.

The four-year-old begins to realize that other children are people apart from him; like him in some ways and different in others. He is discovering that these children have thoughts and feelings and ideas just as he does, and that they have a mother and father and a family life, too. He likes to say, "Tommy's mommy makes cookies," as if to boast that he understands about other families. He may enjoy knowing Tommy's parents and visiting in their home, but he is very certain that no home is as good as his own.

In spite of his pride in home and family, the four-year-old is often not a joy to his older brothers and sisters; he can be a big nuisance to them, spoiling their games with clowning or complaining. The siblings younger than he do not fare much better. They are often pushed and scolded for being unable to play with him on his terms.

At age four (with adult encouragement), brushing teeth, washing hands and face, dressing and undressing and going to the toilet alone have all become a normal part of the child's day. He can lace his shoes, but tying them is still beyond his ability.

The curious four-year-old

The four-year-old child likes to go to the bathroom with friends, for he is curious to see whether they have the same body parts and habits as he. When visiting a new home, he often asks to see the bathroom. This is part of natural growing up and increasing awareness of the world about him. Parents can comfort themselves that this is a normal curiosity, yet wisely give a bit of unobtrusive supervision to the visits.

If the youngsters spend too much time observing each other's toilet habits, or begin to inspect each other's genital organs with touching and giggling, the mother can calmly suggest, "Toilet time is over. Come and play with your toys." Without scolding or shaming the children, mother is helping the little ones understand that there is a limit to bathroom play.

Many nursery schools are aware of the small child's natural curiosity and his need to learn about others, so have wisely arranged one lavatory to be used by children of both sexes. In this normal setting, with a relaxed teacher near by, the small one has the opportunity of learning about himself and those of the opposite sex. He soon learns that he can ask the teacher anything that he does not understand or that disturbs him.

Little Alice, an only child who had had no previous opportunities to learn about the differences between boys and girls, went to her teacher bewildered.

ALICE: *What's that thing Billy has that squirts water?*
TEACHER: *Where is Billy squirting water?*
ALICE: *There (pointing to lavatory).*
TEACHER: *Show me where he squirted the water.*

When they reached the lavatory, Alice showed where Billy had stood, right in front of a toilet.

TEACHER: *Why, Billy was going to the toilet. He is a boy, and he stands up to urinate.*
ALICE: *Why?*
TEACHER: *Boys stand up to go to the toilet, because they have a penis. The urine comes through their penis.*
ALICE: *I don't have one of those.*

TEACHER: *No, only boys and men have a penis. Girls and women sit on the toilet to urinate. Did you remember to wash your hands when you were through using the toilet?*
ALICE: *No, I forgot. I'll wash them now.*

Soon Alice was deeply involved in making as many soapsuds as possible, as she washed her hands. Alice was learning new things all the time, so the new part of a boy's anatomy was no more startling or unusual than learning to use the new school paints or discovering that Mary had a twin sister.

Group play

After many months of parallel play with his friends, the four-year-old is learning the joy of cooperative play. At three, when he played airplane with his friends, all would go zooming about independently. They would play near each other, but each airplane was off on his own adventure. At four, the airplanes begin to plan their strategy; they all go in a straight line, they all dip and rise at the same time, and they all land to let out their passengers. A lead airplane is often chosen to head the formation.

Boys and girls still play easily together, but on occasion several boys will find a mutual activity and band together. Girls, too, will discover that dollhouse play runs happily with several girls. At times the boy and girl groups will taunt each other with, "You can't play with us!" or some similar chant, demonstrating that awareness of sex differences is beginning.

Dramatic play

The four-year-old is a real ham! His dramatic play shows great imagination. House, store, train, doctor, dentist, and hospital all bring out the actor in him, and with a few costumes and props this play can last a long time (with time out for tattling, quarreling, and sometimes a good hand-slapping fight).

Many parents are chagrined when they listen to their children play house. The little mother scolds and shakes her doll babies, she forces them to eat and spanks them soundly for crying. The play fathers are often tyrants who read the paper and demand dinner when not bossing their children. Many a mother wonders if her child has this picture of her. What the four-year-old is doing is enjoying the authority he has in his dramatic play. Pretending to be mother, father, or teacher suddenly makes him all-wise, all-powerful, and he gets carried away with his role.

The four-year-old's dramatic flair is natural for him at this age, for he does not live a calm, quiet existence. It seems at times that everything is explosive. At the dinner table he is apt to put on a dramatic production, refusing all food because mother expects him to eat cooked carrots, when everyone knows he wants them raw. It becomes a part of some children's dinnertime that about half-way through the meal they have to leave immediately for the bathroom. This often brings adult scolding and childish tears. If a parent can remember that this is a habit of many children, his reaction is more tolerant toward his own child.

Stress reactions

Vomiting when too many restrictions are placed on him, or when his day is not going right for him, is not unusual with some little ones. Some children complain of a stomachache during times of stress. Some need to urinate. One mother was concerned because when she needed to scold her child, he always cried and demanded to go immediately to the toilet. If she did not let him run off to the bathroom, he had an accident. She was sure he did it on purpose, and this infuriated her. These reactions to stress are quite common in some children. With parent calmness and patience, they usually change as the child matures. To scold, shame, or draw attention to the child's reaction merely heightens his need to have this response and prolongs it.

A second-grade teacher discovered that almost every year she had one or two children who still had this reaction to stress.

A seven-year-old girl ran around the classroom (which she knew was not good classroom behavior) and bumped into an easel, knocking down several jars of tempera paint. When the children heard the noise and saw the mess on the floor, a big gasp went up, and then—dead silence. The teacher waited until she could say calmly, "We will need to ask Mr. Adams to come with his pail and mop to clean up the paint. Please find him and ask him to come."

The little girl, clutching herself, whined, "I have to go to the toilet, now!" It was just a little of that four-year-old reaction left over. The teacher excused the child to go to the lavatory, and when she returned said kindly, "Now you are ready to call Mr. Adams. We are lucky that we have such a good helper. Would you like to have Mary go with you?" The little girl needed no scolding, for she knew her running had caused the accident. She was helped to meet the situation by doing something to correct the result of her carelessness. When the spilled paint was removed and the custodian duly thanked, the little girl went to her teacher and whispered to her that she was sorry. "I know you are, for you're a fine girl," answered the teacher with a little love-pat on the girl's shoulder. "Now sit in your seat and we'll get back to work."

Had the teacher scolded the child for wanting to go to the toilet and accused her of trying to avoid an unpleasant situation, the need to urinate would have been accented once more in the child's mind and reaction.

The teacher was wise enough to know that children often have strange reactions in times of stress.

Noise

Today's child lives in a world of noise. Home used to be a peaceful haven, but many homes today are reminiscent of the practice studios in music colleges; different sounds come from each room. Many mothers turn on the radio when they wake in the morning and turn it off the last thing at night. They defend the habit by saying the music makes their work easier, and that the friendly-voiced disk jockeys are cheering. Father may be running his hi-fi, and Junior is listening to the latest adventure on TV, while big brother is walking around with a faraway expression on his face and one ear plugged into his pocket radio, which is broadcasting a baseball game. No wonder some little ones grow nodules on their vocal cords from too much loud, strained talking. How else can they be heard? Others soon learn that no one is really listening to them—so why talk?

Blessed is the child who has a mother and father who listen, really listen, to him.

Listening

The parents who listen hear the child's fears and his questions. They learn when their child is under deep stress, when he needs help to understand a situation, when he is happy and wants someone to rejoice with him. If a parent tunes in to his child, many heartbreaks can be avoided and a helping hand can be offered when needed.

Parents' not-hearing ears are all too common. A small child whose parents don't listen learns that no one really cares about his problems and joys. If he cries and screams loud enough, he gets attention. Even the scolding or spanking he gets for bad behavior is better than being ignored. Parents complain that their child is exasperating and will not mind them, even though they scold, punish, and spank. The children often get immune to all the punishment and seem to seek more, through being obstreperous. Exasperating your parents is better than having them ignore you or not care about you.

At the other extreme is the parent who talks too much, never giving the child an opportunity to finish what he wants to tell or ask. They complete the child's sentence if he hesitates. They beat him to the draw every time.

"Tommy, say thank-you to Grandma for the present. Tell her how much you like it." Poor Tommy had thought of thanking his grandmother all by himself, but Mother had to grab the limelight once again and do the directing.

The parent who clings to every word the child says, as though each word were a precious pearl, puts undue emphasis upon the child's rights. Regardless of who is talking to her, if her child rudely interrupts the adult speaking, the mother turns from the unfinished sentence of the adult and listens to her child. That is a foolproof way to teach your child that he is always first and most important, dwarfing adults by comparison. Naturally the shunted adult, in turn, loves Mother's "little monster."

The mother would still be "listening" to her child when he bursts into an adult conversation if she said kindly, "Just a minute, Jimmy. Grandfather was in the midst of telling me something interesting." Then, giving Jimmy a pleasant look and putting a restraining hand on his shoulder, she would return her attention to Grandfather. When Grandfather finished his thought, she could turn to the child and say, "Now, what is it you want to tell me?"

This child would know that Mother cares and listens to him, and he would also learn that Grandfather is important and should have his turn without being interrupted.

Teaching modesty

The four-year-old child is learning to be more independent. He is no longer next to mother or father or another adult for most of his day. He is now able to play alone in a room or in his yard. He can learn to be content in a nursery school, knowing that he will return to his own home later. Mother can now dress in privacy and should start teaching her child that there are times when she prefers to be alone. She may ask her child to wait outside the bathroom door, as she closes it after her. At this age it is best if children see other nude children rather than adults. We must teach children not only about the anatomy of a human being, but also respect for people's privacy and a wholesome modesty about themselves.

It can be suggested to a four- or five-year-old that "now that you're getting much older and can take care of yourself in the bathroom, you don't need to tell everyone that you're going to the toilet. If you want to tell someone, come and tell me softly." He can begin to learn that some activities are private. Care must be taken that he is never shamed or embarrassed because he forgets and announces his intention to urinate. The difference between modesty and shame is great!

Questions about babies

Being alert to children's questions and comments gives adults the clue to the teaching of facts at the times when they will best be received. Most sex education is carried on in this way with the small child. Thus many

four-year-old children who have been told a number of
times that a baby grows in mother's uterus within her
body will see a new baby and ask once again:

CHILD: Where did Mrs. Smith get that baby?
ADULT: The baby grew in a special place in her body,
called the uterus (or womb).
CHILD: How did it get in the mommy?
ADULT: It grew from a tiny egg cell which is in all women's bodies. When a cell from the father joined the egg, a
new baby started to grow.
CHILD: How did the baby get out?

At this point it is often good to ask the child how he
thinks it got out. His answer is often most unusual, and
the adult should take care not to laugh. Many small
children get the idea that the baby came out through
the navel.

If the child doesn't know, or has the wrong idea, tell
him as clearly as possible.

ADULT: There is a very special path called the vagina,
that the baby comes out through. We call it a birth canal.
When it's time for the baby to be born, the vagina stretches
like a rubber balloon, big enough for the baby to get
through. It only stretches big when a baby is ready to be
born.
CHILD: Where does it come out?
ADULT: The opening is between the mother's legs.
CHILD: Is that how I got out?
ADULT: Yes, that's how you were born.
CHILD: Show me where I came out.
ADULT: When a mother isn't having a baby, you can't
see the hallway. Pieces of skin cover it.

These same questions often are asked of the nursery
school teacher. She can answer the child in much the
same way. Also, there is always a child who volunteers
his incorrect version. The teacher should grasp the opportunity to tell the correct story of birth.

Misconceptions about birth

Many parents tell their children that the baby grows in mother's tummy. Horrors! What a place to grow in, when you remember some of the garbage we human beings eat and the poisons we drink! Another favorite explanation is that "You grew in a little nest right under my heart." A lovely, poetic thought in the mother's mind, but the child undoubtedly visualizes a bird's nest with the baby's mouth open wide, begging for food.

Many adults today remember their parents' tall tales about new babies and where they came from. In Grandmother's day, the question was often firmly answered with, "The doctor brought the baby in his black bag." The baby was born at home in those days, with the doctor or midwife arriving shortly before the event. Most children believed the story without question. There were no radio or television broadcasts to shake their faith in their parents' word; no magazines or newspapers dared to enter homes with sex in the headlines.

In mother's day it was quite common to be told you were found under a cabbage, or were a gift from Heaven that the stork dropped off.

Many young adults of today have learned early in life that their mother's flippant answer, "We bought you at the store," was untrue, and most of their sex information and misinformation has been obtained from their peers, from newspapers, magazines, or even "girly" magazines. Some parents have told their children that they grew in their mother's body, but education stopped firmly at this point.

Today's child and birth information

Today's child needs to know the whole story—and will know, whether he hears it at home or from other sources. Sex is no longer a taboo subject. It is flagrantly headlined in stories of the sex deviate. "Sexiness" is acclaimed by many as their goal.

Schools, churches, and most parents are deeply concerned about existing problems and want their children to have a happy, contented, and good life, and to have respect and reverence for the wondrous story of the creation of life. We start by being honest with our children. We must help them find contentment in their sex, help them to learn about their own and the opposite sex, about the miracle of life, and to respect their own and other people's bodies and personal rights.

One of the most important elements in teaching sex and in helping children to develop good attitudes is the example set by their parents and teachers.

Religion and sex education

All of sex education can be related to religion when the situation is appropriate. In homes where religion guides the families in their daily lives, in churches and parochial schools that teach religion as part of their educational curriculum, there will certainly be the desire to help children see God's plan for people, as interpreted by their particular religious faith.

When children are taught the story of Creation, they learn that God made man and woman, and He gave them the ability to bring new life into the world. Learning how God provided for the reproduction of all plant and animal life is a wonderful story for children to learn. Adults can help them understand that their bodies and lives are gifts from God, to use in a way pleasing to Him.

In telling a child about the development and growth of a baby within the mother's uterus, he can be helped to see it in the light of his religion.

CHILD: *I like the story you told me about how babies are made.*

ADULT: *It is the story of a miracle. Most everyone refers to the birth of a baby as the miracle of birth.*
CHILD: *It really is a miracle 'cause a baby starts out smaller than a dot and then grows into a real live baby.*
ADULT: *God has made the miracle possible.*

It is good to point out to children that in spite of the amazing strides man has made in science and industry, never has he been able to invent a machine that can produce a live baby. God has so created the body of a man and a woman that a man has the ability to start new life and a woman has the capacity to grow a baby in her uterus.

Through conversations with children, adults can place religious emphasis upon the reproduction of plants and animals and people. In discussing the need for plants and the many ways they reproduce, children may be told, "God has given us the amazing world in which we live. He has made it possible for all plants to reproduce, assuring us the food and materials we need for all our days on the earth."

When talking about the birth of a human being to children, some parents and parochial teachers will wish to emphasize that "A baby is God's gift to a husband and wife. The bodies of the husband and wife are made in such a way that together they are able to grow babies. God has made it possible for them to have children."

Religion can give an added dimension to children's appreciation and respect for all life.

Chapter Four

Age Five

The five-year-old child

The five-year-old child is no longer tied to his mother's apron strings, yet to him she continues to be the great and wise queen of his world. He has reached the age where he can go happily to kindergarten and looks forward to this half-day separation from home. He often falls madly in love with his kindergarten teacher; she may be the first "mother-figure" he has ever had the opportunity to get to know well, besides his own mother. After he is well entrenched in kindergarten life, he often goes home and quotes firmly, "Miss Green says . . . ," as though they were words straight from Heaven. He is impressed with this new authority and wants to share it with his family. Many children take their teacher's every suggestion literally and accept it as law.

One day Miss Green said to the children, "If Mother has a little cardboard box she can spare, will you bring it to school tomorrow so we can use it for our art work?" To little Mary this meant one thing, and that was to show up the next day with a little cardboard box. When her mother could not find one, she burst into tears and declared her teacher would not accept her without the box.

Age five is more agile than four, can use crayons with greater assurance, and is able to draw a recognizable man. He is usually able to talk without infantile articulation. He is gaining a more stable reaction to everyday happenings and delights his family with his seriousness, desire to learn, and his new poise. He even says "Please" and "Thank you"!

Playmates

The five-year-old child prefers playmates to solitary play, and chooses play groups of two to five children. He may still hold dear his imaginary friends.

The five-year-old child makes little distinction between sexes in play, but is beginning to choose different toys. Boys of this age choose trucks, cars, tools, and blocks, but will also join the girls for playing house or hospital. The girls usually choose dolls, dollhouses, dollhouse toys, and costumes for dress-up as their favorite playthings, but they can also enjoy block building or hammering with the boys. Little by little, children begin to show their sex differences.

The five-year-old child usually becomes more modest, and there is a decrease in sex play. Most children of this age are aware of the physical differences between the sexes, yet when questioned about how they can tell which are boys and which are girls, they are apt to say the clothes or haircut tell the difference.

Reactions to tension

At five, many children pick up strange little habits such as nose-picking, eye-blinking, sniffing, and even thumb-sucking. Tense or anxious moments usually do not cause vomiting or urinating, as they did a year ago, but are now met with restless behavior—often twisting or pulling at clothes and buttons.

Being boys and girls

Although boys and girls still play as happily with the opposite sex as with their own, they often begin to identify more and more with their own sex. Parents can do much to help their children in this area. Even children's names help them to be accepted by other children. A boy named Carol has a hard time in life, for the name is so commonly attached to a girl. He is often the target of jokes.

Mothers who yearned for a baby girl will sometimes dress their little boy in feminine clothes, and cannot bear to cut off his beautiful curly hair. Even at four and five years of age, these children are made to suffer from the taunting of other children or thoughtlessly cruel remarks made by adults.

Boys should look like boys and girls should like like girls at an early age. It is true that little girls' legs are better protected in overalls when they are playing, but manufacturers make feminine-looking overalls and slacks, too.

Fathers and mothers also help their children by demonstrating their happiness in having the child be the sex he is. Letting the little girl know that a girl is nice to have, that she looks lovely in her dresses, and that her feminine hair style is attractive, helps her to accept her sex.

In the same manner, a boy must also feel that being a boy is desirable. Accepting his rough-and-tumble type of play with good humor gives him a chance to demonstrate that he is a boy.

"Crushes" and fantasies

The small child often gets a "crush" on the parent of the opposite sex. He will have fantasies about his relationship with his parents. A little girl may dream about marrying her father. She sees herself cooking and keeping house for him, just the way Mother does. There are times when she wishes her mother were gone, or even dead, so she could have her father all to herself. This does not mean she does not love her mother dearly, but that her fantasy has grown to the place where Mother seems to be in the way. She will realize at other times that the wish to have Mother out of the way is wicked, and will feel woefully guilty about having such feelings.

A little boy also may have fantasies, but about his mother. He, too, will dream of marrying Mother and having her all to himself; he, too, will wish Father gone and then have the resultant anxiety.

These fantasies are not unusual for children of this age. However, the parent should try to help the child avoid such dreams as are unrealistic and help him to gain a true understanding of his own role in the family.

Mother should never call her son "my little man" or "my lover," for these names suggest to the child that he is more than her son. By the same token, a father should not refer to his daughter as "my little mother" or "my sweetheart." These terms of endearment should be reserved for his wife.

Allowing a child to slip into the parents' bed also starts these fantasy dreams. If a child has a bad dream and comes to the parents' bed, pleading to crawl into bed with mother or father, his request should be denied. The mother or father should get up, take the child to his room, show him that there is no danger in the room, and then tuck him lovingly back into his own bed.

The mother should not listen to her child's plea to "lie down next to me for a few minutes." If he really needs cuddling to get over the fright, sit in a chair to do it. The father should never get out of his bed to let the frightened child in. From the beginning, the child should be made to know that father and mother are man and wife, and that children do not interfere with this. They need also to learn that they are dearly loved as son or daughter and can depend on their parents for protection and comfort. Parents' firmness about not sharing their bed with their child will help him learn his true place in the family, and avoid the anxiety that results from fantasies.

Masturbation

Masturbation (feeling or rubbing one's own sex organs) may continue with some kindergarten-aged children. The parent should try to avoid attracting attention to the act and be especially careful that the child does not feel the parent is emotionally upset by the masturbating, lest guilt feelings develop within the child. The feelings of guilt and wrongdoing will draw undue attention to the act, and this emotional stress may result in the child's feeling more and more compelled to masturbate. The guilt feelings may also affect his future attitude toward sexual intercourse in marriage.

Many adults have heard untrue wives' tales about masturbation. Every conceivable illness or disorder has been blamed on masturbation, such as becoming impotent, bald, or having skin problems. All these tales are untrue. There is no physical damage done by masturbating, but emotional disturbances may develop unless the problem is approached wisely by the parents. All children at one time or another have rubbed or manipulated their sex organs. As they grow older and become more involved in play and other activities, as they become more social and gain assurance that they are securely loved by their family (and that they in turn can love others), the desire to masturbate becomes less and less.

If a kindergarten child actively masturbates, there are things parents can do to help him. First of all, make a point of showing the child that he is greatly loved. A child who feels unloved often will turn his love to himself, and masturbating is proving to himself that he "feels good"—a form of self-love. Never send a child to bed as punishment, for he will seek some consolation for his anger and hurt feelings. Masturbating with fantasies is consoling to a child who feels hurt and lonely.

If a parent is aware that his child is playing with his genital organs under the blanket, he could say calmly, "Put your arms over the blanket. That will help you go to sleep. You are playing with your penis [or vulva for a girl] and that will keep you from going to sleep. Now it is sleeping time."

A child should be taught to get up as soon as he wakes in the morning, and encouraged to go to sleep quickly at night. Many parents complain that their children take hours to go to sleep. Parents can do much to help children to relax and fall asleep quickly.

A quiet period before bedtime is essential for good relaxation. This eliminates radio, television, and exciting stories. Vigorous exercise during the day aids sleep, but roughhousing before going to bed is too stimulating. Regularity of the bedtime is very important for most children. After checking to be sure that a child has finished his bath, urinated, had a small drink, said his prayers, and is comfortably tucked into bed, the parent should leave the room and not allow any nonsense. A child must know that parents have a firm rule, which they enforce, about getting out of bed, singing, playing, or calling to parents for "just one more drink, or . . ." A permissive parent encourages the child to become more and more creative about ways to keep his family aware of his presence and keep himself awake. Some children will do almost anything to keep parents near. Complaining of a stomachache, even vomiting if necessary, is not unusual for these children. If parents permit this behavior to change their rules, they are encouraging the child's bad habit to persist, not helping him to gain security and independence.

Parents, too, can be creative in helping children relax and fall asleep quickly. One mother discovered that her child was taking longer and longer to get to sleep, and although she caused no problem to the parents, she was often still awake when they retired. One night she entered her daughter's room and talked to her about it.

MOTHER: *You're supposed to be asleep and you're still awake. Sleep is important and makes people feel good. You're not going to sleep because you are dreaming a little play in your mind. When I was your age, I used to dream little plays.*

CHILD: *You did! What kind of plays did you dream?*

MOTHER: *Oh, there were many different kinds, but they were always about me. Sometimes I would dream that I was so great that everyone did just what I wanted them to do. My plays got too long sometimes, and kept me awake, which wasn't good.*

CHILD: *My plays are long, too.*

MOTHER: *I have an idea. Each night we'll let you have ten minutes to dream your play. Then I'll come in and take a pretty handkerchief and lay it across your eyes. That will be the curtain going down on your play. Then you will stop your play and go to sleep. The next night you can go on with your play.*

CHILD: *I'll forget where I left off.*

MOTHER: *That's true. I have an idea. You tell me where you stopped. I'll remember and remind you the next night.*

CHILD: *I like that game. Can we start tonight?*

MOTHER: *Yes, but you must remember the rules. Ten minutes, and when the curtain goes down, the play is over and you go to sleep.*

The mother reported that her game went on for months. The child used the crutch of the handkerchief to blot out daydreams and learned to go to sleep within minutes.

Some children feel more secure at night if their bedroom door is ajar and they can hear the usual household noises. Others go to sleep more quickly with a small night light on in the adjoining hall or room.

Ideally, the small child should have his own bedroom. If this is not possible and he must share a room with another child, he should at least have his own bed and sleep alone. Children should never sleep in their parents' room. The child may appear to be asleep, but that is no guarantee that he is. The sounds and movements from his parents' bed may cause him much anxiety.

The new baby

A kindergarten child is usually deeply interested in other people's little babies and may ask if his family can have a baby. It pleases most parents to learn that Junior is anxious to have an addition to the family, and so they tell him the good news as soon as they themselves know.

Some parents spend most of mother's pregnancy preparing Junior. He is told that the newcomer will be his baby, too, and that he can help Mother take care of him. He is told how happy everyone will be when that wonderful bundle of joy arrives. As the parents continue to paint an idyllic picture of the coming event, Junior's mind may become more and more turbulent, and he may have many doubts about the future intruder. This new baby sounds so perfect, he fears that he himself will be completely overshadowed. Junior begins to feel sure that his parents will love the new, perfect baby more than they love him.

There are times when Junior must forego the pleasure of a trip to the zoo, or a bus ride to the beach, because Mother is tired. "She needs her rest these days, because the baby growing in her uterus is getting so big," Junior is told. If he complains bitterly about the great injustice to him, he is scolded and told that he is selfish and that he had better learn to think of others, for soon his mother will have even less time for him. This leaves him angrier than ever and shows him that his foreboding about this baby is true. Junior becomes more and more demanding to prove to himself that his parents have already changed their allegiance to that unborn sibling. In fact, that baby in Mother's body is so big that it already fills Mother's lap, and he has to sit on the chair beside her!

He is learning to resent the whole idea more and more. In his anger he dreams of ways to change the pending event. He may manipulate his daydreams in such a way as to imagine that Mother might fall so hard on her fat stomach that the baby would be killed! He may even plan ways to get rid of the baby in case it survives the fall. He may scheme to throw it out of the window, sure that it will then be dead and gone.

A little girl of five, who had just such daydreams about getting rid of the coming baby, calmly accepted the news when told that their premature baby had died. Soon, however, her earlier dreams of ridding herself of the baby began to disturb her and she convinced herself that she had killed the baby. She started to have serious problems socially and emotionally. She alternated between being an extremely loving and an exceedingly angry child. When she reached first grade she resisted all teaching and refused to enter into any learning situations. She became a nuisance to the rest of the class. Her parents, completely frustrated by their daughter's changed personality, sought professional help. The girl was gradually helped to understand and handle her own problem.

Parents should be as honest as possible with their children in preparing them for a new child. There is no reason to share the news with them the minute the new baby is conceived. Nine months is a long time to wait. When mother starts to expand noticeably, it is soon enough to tell them. In fact, the five-year-old usually does not notice his mother's enlarged body unless he is told about it.

When the pregnant mother is tired or does not feel well, do not blame the unborn baby. A little child will remember and magnify the many times that the baby interfered with his life. He can understand that Mother is tired and does not need to place the blame on anyone.

Let children know that there will be times when the family will be thrilled and happy with the new baby. There will also be times when he will be a big nuisance; sometimes he will cry at dinnertime and spoil everyone's pleasure in eating together. The baby will make a lot of extra work for Mother and Father.

Why do parents want another child if this is true, the children may ask. They can be told that a man and wife should want children. It is their responsibility, pleasure, and privilege to have a good family. Mother and Father love each other very much and want to have children to love. Even though children cause parents much extra work, the joy they receive from their children far outweighs the burden.

Let the children know that there may be times when they will resent the baby's demands and the time devoted to him; let them know that resentment is a normal feeling, but that something can and should be done about it. Parents may wish to tell their children, "When you feel neglected or unhappy after the baby arrives, tell me about it. I'll give you a special time all your own, and we can talk about things." Knowing that they will not be left completely out of the picture reassures the children and helps them visualize themselves in the new situation. They can feel secure that they will continue to get their parents' attention and love.

Small children need to be told many times about

their mother's pending trip to the hospital for the birth of the baby. They must know what will happen to them when Mother is gone. They can plan to have a telephone session with Mother each day that she is in the hospital. They must know that Mother will come back in a few days. Many mothers find that play-acting the scene of going to the hospital over and over with their little children is the best way to prepare them for the actual occurrence. The time taken to prepare and involve children in the birth of a new baby will help them face life realistically and with greater security. It will also prepare them to share in their parents' joy in receiving the newest member of the family.

Questions about babies

Most five-year-old children are only interested in knowing where a baby comes from, and do not ask how the baby started to grow. These children are satisfied with the simple answer, "The baby grows in a special baby-growing place, called a uterus, in Mother's body." They do not need to be told about the egg cell and sperm cell, for it will only confuse them.

Some children of this age, however, do ask more questions and appear to be ready for additional information.

CHILD: *How did the baby get in the mommy to grow?*
MOTHER: *It started from an egg cell.*
CHILD: *Do you have an egg cell in you?*
MOTHER: *Yes, all grown-up ladies have egg cells.*
CHILD: *Will your egg cell grow a baby now?*
MOTHER: *When a sperm cell from Father joins the egg cell, a baby will grow. Right now a baby is not growing in my uterus.*
CHILD: *Why?*
MOTHER: *Because right now Father and I are busy with the children we have. Maybe some other year we can have a baby.*

It is rare for children of this age to ask how the sperm cell gets to the egg cell. If a child should ask such a question, the parent or adult must be ready to answer him. This is the question most adults fear to answer and try to dodge, if possible. A five-year-old child will not be shocked, for his knowledge and understanding are too limited to fully grasp your answer.

CHILD: How does the daddy cell get to the egg cell?

ADULT: When Father shows Mother how much he loves her, he sometimes puts a sperm cell in her body for the egg cell.

CHILD: How does he do it?

ADULT: The sperm cell goes through a very special tube in the penis and enters the mother's vagina. Fathers and mothers do this when they want to have a new child of their very own to love and care for.

CHILD: Can we have a baby?

ADULT: Susie is only a year old. She's our baby.

CHILD: But I want a little-bitsy baby.

ADULT: Someday we may have a new baby, but not now.

Another question often asked is, "Will the baby be a boy or a girl?" It is good for children to know that parents have no choice and that they are happy to receive a child of either sex. A parent may wish to answer this question by saying, "Mothers and fathers never know if the new baby will be a boy or a girl. It makes waiting for the baby exciting, for we don't know which kind of baby it will be. We like both girls and boys, and we will be happy with either kind."

Another question parents may be asked by the five-year-old is, "How does the baby get out of your body?" A truthful answer, told simply along the lines suggested on page 32, will be accepted by the child. "There is a special birth canal for the baby to come out. It's called the vagina." "Where is that place?" some will ask. "When a baby is ready to be born, the birth canal stretches big enough for the baby to go through. Then it comes out a special opening between the mother's legs," the young child can be told. If he wants to see the place, the mother can say, "When a baby is not being born, the place is covered with flaps of skin." If the child persists, he can be answered firmly with, "No, I won't show you. But I'll draw you a picture, so you'll know." A simple sketch will satisfy him.

A parent should not be surprised if a child suddenly pulls her doll from between her legs, to dramatize the birth of a baby. It is usually best to ignore this play.

Sex play

Even though some children show less interest in sex play at this age, others may still be curious. It is not unusual for a five-year-old child to want to see his playmates without clothing. They will often devise doctor or hospital games to legitimize the inspection. This game is usually played behind closed doors. The very secrecy of the game is a sign that children sense that it is inappropriate play. This sexual stimulation should not be encouraged and should not continue, for the child usually has feelings of anxiety about it.

Whenever children are behind closed doors too long and are too quiet or giggly, a parent should investigate. If the adult finds the children disrobed and looking very guilty, it is difficult for even a well-informed parent to avoid being emotional about it. No good can come from emotional outbursts such as "What's the matter with you?" "Aren't you ashamed to be standing there with your clothes off?" "Who taught you to play that dirty game?" "You go home this minute, Jimmy, and don't come back!" "Wait until I tell your mother what you've been doing!" "You should be ashamed of yourselves."

Each child's guilty conscience is enough punishment. They do need, however, a parent's authority to stop the

game and are usually relieved to have the decision made
for them. A firm suggestion that they get dressed and
find something else to do often sees an end to such play.
If, however, the child again becomes involved, he should
be told again in a calm, unblaming way to change the
game. Then at a later time he can be spoken to privately and told firmly that he is not to play such a game,
nor to allow other children to inspect or touch his sex
organs. The adult should set the limits for a child and
enforce them.

Parents should remember that bathroom play is a
common experience of early childhood, and knowing
this should approach the correction of it calmly.

Kindergarten—unit on family

Part of making a good adjustment in life is to be content with one's own sex. The kindergarten teacher is
in a good position to help little children learn about
themselves and others—to help them gain respect for
themselves and their own and the opposite sex. One
teacher used the doll corner as a starting place for a
study of the family. She asked the question, "What is
a boy?" She remembered the answers of the children
and wrote them down. The next day, when all the children were gathered together for sharing time, the
teacher said, "Yesterday I asked the children who were
playing house to tell me what a boy is. They had such
good ideas that I wrote them on this sheet of paper.
I'll read them to you."

"A boy wears pants."
"A boy is a son."
"He is a brother, too."
"A boy likes trains."
"A boy will be a daddy when he grows up."
"A boy is not a girl."
"A boy gets haircuts."

"A boy was a baby when he was little."

Listening to these sentences gave the children more ideas about the characteristics of a boy, and they added to the list. Naturally the girls wanted a story written about them, too. The teacher wrote the sentences about a boy on a large chart and the girls' characteristics on another chart.

The children drew pictures of boys and girls and cut them out and pasted them on the charts. They asked the teacher to read the charts over and over. Soon a few children volunteered to "read" them.

The next member of the family to be written about and discussed was Mother. Naturally the first sentence was, "A mother has babies." They discovered that a mother is a wife, and once upon a time she was even a girl, and a baby.

Father, baby, grandmother, grandfather, uncle, aunt, and cousin—all were studied. The children enjoyed learning and telling how all these people fit into their family. Some children learned for the first time that one grandmother was Father's mother, and the other grandmother was Mother's mother. These children seemed to have been under the impression that grandparents were just there to be their grandparents. How surprising it was to learn that Grandmother had once been a baby, then a girl, a wife, a mother who had Daddy (or Mother) as her baby. Now she is a grandmother. The children were encouraged to bring pictures of the family members, and a bulletin board was filled with pictures labeled "Jimmy's Grandfather," "Mary and Her Father," "Dean's New Baby Sister."

One child brought a recent family picture (taken at a family reunion) of grandmother and grandfather in the center of the picture, with their sons and daughters on either side. The sons-in-law and daughters-in-law were also in the picture, with their sons and daughters in front of them. The teacher said, "Lisa, your family picture tells a story. Would you like to hear the story?"

Lisa and the other children eagerly asked to hear it, so the teacher began, "Once upon a time there was a little baby girl who grew up and became a lovely young lady. There was also a little baby boy and he grew up to be a strong, fine young man. He met the lovely young lady and soon discovered that he loved her very much. He asked the young lady if she would marry him and become his wife. So the young lady and man were married, and that is how Lisa's grandmother and grandfather became a family. The young husband and wife were very happy, but after a while they wished they had a baby. So one day a beautiful healthy baby boy was born. Now there were three people in their family, and the young wife and husband were now a mother and father, too." As the teacher told her story, she indicated the people in the picture. Pointing to one of the men she said, "This son grew up and was married, and here is his wife. Can you guess what happiness came to them?"

The children all called out, "A baby! A beautiful baby!" When the teacher pointed to Lisa's parents, how exciting it was for them to say, "A baby! A beautiful baby was born, and her name is Lisa!"

The teacher ended her story by saying, "The first young man and lady are many years older now. They are mother and father to their big sons and daughters and to their sons-in-law and daughters-in-law. They are grandmother and grandfather to all the children their sons and daughters have. They look at all the people in their family, and the man says to his wife, 'See our wonderful children and grandchildren. What a fine, big family we have!' he adds with a proud smile."

As the children learned more and more about a family, they had new interest in their own family. Their parents and grandparents were made to tell their stories. The children learned that it took a man and woman to start the family unit; that from them the children grew and were born. They gained a new understanding of the importance of the female and the male. A little boy said with pride, "I'm a boy, and I'll grow up and be a daddy and go to work." The girls were equally impressed with their roles as female members of the family.

Many of the children made booklets about their families. The pictures showed a mother, with the word "Mother" laboriously written by the small hand of the artist. Father, sister, brother, grandmother, and all members of the family were included, often sharing the limelight with a family dog or parakeet. As the children showed their books to each other, they discovered that not all families were exactly alike. Mary's grandmother had died, John's father did not live at his home anymore, Elizabeth had a maid living with her family, and Tommy did not have any pets because the apartment had a rule about pets.

Kindergarten—new babies

The study of the family also started discussions about new babies or expected babies. The kindergarten teacher encouraged the children to tell about the babies they had or were expecting in their family.

Elizabeth announced proudly, "We are going to have a baby in a week or a month."

"How do you know?" challenged a youngster.

"'Cause my mommy's pregnant, and the doctor said the baby'll come soon," answered Elizabeth, proudly.

The teacher said, "How wonderful your news is, Elizabeth! I imagine it's hard for you to wait. Can anyone tell me what it means for a mother to be pregnant?"

"I know," shouted Elizabeth. "When a baby is growing in Mommy's stomach, she's pregnant!"

"Yes, Elizabeth, when a new baby is growing in

mother's body, she is pregnant. The baby doesn't grow in mother's stomach. That's where the food she eats goes. The baby grows in a special baby-growing place called the uterus. The uterus is used only for growing babies," explained the teacher.

The interest in babies was high, and so children drew pictures of babies and told stories about babies. The teacher provided some old magazines, and some children cut out all the pictures of babies they could find and made a baby scrapbook. Under some of the pictures the children dictated short stories for the teacher to write. Without saying anything to the children, the teacher told Elizabeth's mother about their study of the family and invited her to visit school. Elizabeth's mother casually dropped in one morning to see the charts and scrapbooks the children had made. Elizabeth told her little friends, "This is my mommy. She's pregnant. Remember?"

Some of the children talked to Elizabeth's mother and asked her questions. Bobby asked, "When is your baby going to be borned?"

"Very soon," replied the mother with a happy smile. "When our baby is born, would you like to see it?"

Later, she brought the baby over on a warm sunny day, while the children were on the playground. She held it up for all the children to see, while they stood quietly around her. It was Bobby who said thoughtfully, "Now you aren't pregnant anymore."

During the study of the family, the kindergarten teacher read stories to the children about families, babies, grandmothers, and grandfathers.*

Kindergarten—animal babies

One day Peter announced that their cat was pregnant. This was a new idea to some children. They had not

* See listing at end of book.

transferred the idea of a human being's pregnancy and birth to animals. One child asked how Peter could tell that the cat was pregnant, and was told rather haughtily by the owner that anyone could see that the cat's sides were fat from having the babies growing inside her.

The pregnant cat, at the teacher's suggestion, was brought over to school one day by Peter's mother for a short visit. As the children sat quietly in their chairs, the cat proceeded to amuse them by rubbing her sides against their legs and jumping on the tables. Peter was asked to tell about his cat. What did she eat, where did she sleep, what tricks did she know, and how old was she?

One child asked where the cat's husband was. Peter explained that cats do not get married, so she did not have a husband. Peter's mother added that the handsome big male cat named Joey, who belonged to their neighbor, was their cat's mate and would be the father of the kittens. The children were relieved and pleased to hear that the baby kittens would have a father.

Several days after the kittens were born, Peter's mother invited the children to visit. The patient mother cat permitted them to inspect her new family and watch them nurse. Peter's mother picked one kitten up and let the children gently touch its warm fur. She pointed out that its eyes were closed because they were not completely developed and the bright lights could harm its eyes. She also drew their attention to how weak its little legs were.

Several weeks later, the kittens paid a short visit to school so that the children could see their growth in size and ability. Of course, the eyes were carefully examined by each child, and they were excited to discover that they could now be seen. Their teacher had told them how the kitten's eyes would slowly open, just a little each day. This was not only a wonderful experience for the children, but involving the parents brought a closer relationship between the school and the home.

Most kindergarten teachers discover that the children do not ask how the kitten got out of the mother cat's body (or a baby from the human being's body). However, occasionally a child may ask. If the teacher prefers, she can tell the child, "I will answer your question after a while, when we finish what we are doing right now." She must be sure then to ask him later, when the other children are busy, to repeat his question. She can answer it in the same way the parent does: "There is a very special birth canal called the vagina, which stretches big enough for the baby to pass through. It opens up between the legs when the kittens are born."

The kindergarten teacher may decide to answer his questions in front of all the children, if she feels they are mature enough and ready to understand. She may also wish to show the film *Kittens' Birth and Growth*, which shows the actual birth of kittens.

Kindergarten—sex pictures

It is not unusual for a kindergarten child to draw a picture of a person and draw in the navel; sometimes a completely dressed figure will sport a navel and a penis, also. It is best to ignore the parts shown in the pictures. If the child mentions, "See the belly button," the teacher may comment that she sees the navel. If he repeats the words "belly button," it may be because he thinks the teacher did not understand. It may then be pointed out to the child that "belly button" is the name very little children sometimes use, but the real name is "navel."

If children giggle at the drawing of a person showing the penis and navel, it is again best to treat it matter-of-factly and brush over it lightly as something not especially important. Studying the next child's picture and finding something good to say about it, will soon focus attention away from the picture that caused the children to laugh.

Kindergarten—parent cooperation

Some teachers may wonder if the parents of their kindergarten children would object to the study of the family and reproduction. Teachers who have conducted units similar to the one just described have found that parents not only did not object, but many made a point of telling the teacher how pleased they were with their child's enthusiasm and reaction to the study.

Chapter Five

Age Six

The six-year-old child

The six-year-old child no longer has Mother as the center of his universe. He has displaced her top position by himself. He can be rude and argumentative with his mother, and may often behave worst with her. Yet he has fears that she may die, or simply not be there when he needs her.

At this age, the child acts as though he knows everything and wants to have his own way in all he does. He seeks to be first in everything; at school he will battle for first position in line regardless of where the line is going. At home he wants to be loved the best of all the children, and expects lavish praise for all he does. First-grade teachers are accustomed to his demands to "See me hang by my knees!" "See my picture!"

Good and bad behavior hold much interest for the six-year-old. As a result, an excessive amount of tattling takes place. The child seems to delight in telling both mother and teacher about the bad thing John or Mary did, though he himself may many times have been guilty of the same thing.

His name has become extremely important to him since he elevated himself to his new, lofty position. For a teacher to make a mistake and call him by another child's name is a cardinal sin which he finds hard to excuse. He likes to see his name on school papers, on a chart or a blackboard. He writes his name on everything he makes and owns. The first-grade teacher often watches with delight as a child paints an unusually good picture at the easel, and plans to display it on the bulletin board. If she does not snatch it quickly, the child is apt to take the brightest-colored paint and boldly write his name in huge letters right over the picture. If the teacher beats the child to the draw and gets the picture before its artist autographs his masterpiece, she may lose the battle after all; he may insist on immediately taking it home. He cannot bear to have the teacher keep it, even though she assures him he may have it when it is taken down from the display wall.

"My mother wants me to take it home," he will argue. Yet his mother often later has a crumpled, torn sheet presented to her. The precious picture does not receive "precious handling" on the way home from school.

The six-year-old child no longer seeks solitary play, but wants a friend or group to join him. A special playmate is important to him. If a third child joins in the play, arguing, tears, or hurt feelings usually result; one of the three children will undoubtedly be excluded.

Leadership begins to be noticed at this time. However, the leader usually has only a small group to lead. It is not unusual for the leader to be very domineering and bossy, much to his parents' dismay. Larger groups of children will play together, but their play is not organized and the rules are so fluid that they hardly seem to be playing together. In fact, a child may join or leave the group and not even be noticed. Not much attention is paid to the sex of the child, if the game is equally interesting to both boys and girls.

Girls continue to enjoy doll play, but it is becoming

more and more involved. Their dolls now need wardrobes, and doll furniture is thoroughly enjoyed. A doll cupboard with dishes, pots, and pans and a stove and refrigerator bring joy to the little mothers. Add a costume box, and much dramatic play takes place. Boys will occasionally join the girls, especially if nothing more interesting presents itself.

Some parents notice that their girls do not enjoy doll play as much as others. This often happens when compatible friends living nearby are not girls, but boys who enjoy more vigorous games. The girl whose closest friends are boys will choose their games rather than solitary play with dolls. Six-year-old boys enjoy running, tumbling, and jumping, and like to shout wildly. War games stimulate them to very dramatic play, with much killing, hiding, capturing, all done to the accompaniment of gun noises and an overabundance of orders. One young "soldier" may be mortally wounded and die a miserable, lonely death dozens of times during the play, only to arise and continue the battle.

Favorite toys include building blocks, cars, trucks and trains. Santa Claus (still firmly believed in by the majority of children) finds that boys choose toys of this type to put on their Christmas lists.

Sex differences

At six there is a marked awareness of sex differences. This often leads to mutual investigation by both sexes. Playing doctor or hospital continues to be the legitimate excuse to view each other's bodies; frequently they will play they are taking rectal temperatures, to see the other child's differences in body structure. Parents who hear this play taking place should step in and stop the game. Emotionalism or anger on the part of the parent will heighten the child's feeling that this play is "off limits," and will undoubtedly make it seem of greater impor-

tance than it is. A firm but unaccusing "Get dressed
and play a different game," suggested by the adult, usually stops the game. The embarrassed faces will tell the
parent that the children realize the game was not a good
one, and they are usually relieved to have the parent
stop their play.

This is a good age once again to plan to have the
child experience seeing the body of a baby. If at all possible, the mother should arrange a casual visit to a
friend's home at a time when the baby is being bathed
and fed. The child's questions should be encouraged
and answered honestly and simply.

GIRL: Why does the baby have that (pointing to the
penis).
MOTHER: Because the baby is a boy. It's called a penis.
All boys and men have a penis.
GIRL: Why?
MOTHER: When little boys go to the toilet, the urine
comes out of the penis.
GIRL: Why don't I have one?
MOTHER: Because you're a girl. No girls or women have
a penis. That's how we can tell if a new baby is a boy or a
girl.

When a boy views a baby girl, his questions will be
similar. He needs to be reassured that the baby girl was
born without a penis and that there is no danger that
he will lose his.

Seeing a baby nurse at the mother's breast is often the
most startling part of the experience. Today's women
make nursing a very private affair. Years ago, when
mothers took their babies with them wherever they
went, it was not unusual to see a mother nurse her baby
at a picnic or even on public transportation. This being
the age of baby-sitters and formulas, children seldom
get to see a mother care for and nurse her baby unless
he is a member of the family. If the child asks questions
about the breasts, he should be answered. If questions

are not forthcoming, the parent should start the conversation.

MOTHER: *See how the little baby drinks his milk.*
CHILD: *Is he drinking milk? Where does it come from?*
MOTHER: *When a mother has a baby, milk comes into the mother's breasts for the baby to drink.*
CHILD: *How does the milk get there?*
MOTHER: *The reason women have breasts is to feed little babies. Milk develops in the breasts when a mother has a new baby. It is warm and sweet and good for the little baby. It will help the baby grow. When the baby is big enough to eat food as you and I do, then milk stops developing in the breasts.*

Seeing the bodies of other children of a similar age is also good, if such an experience comes about through natural circumstance. Having brothers, sisters, visiting friends, or relatives usually provides such an opportunity. Bedtime or dressing time, with a parent nearby, makes a normal and natural way for such learning to take place. If questions arise, the parent is there to answer them.

Learning respect for privacy

Parents should train their child to understand that his parents' bedroom is a private place. It is good to close the door at times and ask the child to knock and wait for an invitation to enter before opening it. In like manner, parents need to observe the same rule before entering the child's room, when the door is closed. Also, by this time a child should know that going to the toilet or bathing are private times, and the closed door should be respected.

When a child is four, five, or six it is best that he not see his parents walking around in the nude. The large, nude body of an adult often disturbs children. To some it is unattractive, while to others it may be sexually over-stimulating. Children often try to get a glimpse of mother or father in the bathroom or while dressing, which is par for the course. This should not cause out-bursts of anger toward the curious child, nor should the parent try quickly to hide his nude body in embarrass-ment. Rather, tell the child that you know he is curious about how an adult looks without his clothes, but that you prefer to be alone when taking a bath. En-courage him to ask you questions, so you can tell him the things he wants to know.

There are families whose homes resemble a nudist colony, and they prefer it that way; however, they will need to teach their children the proper times to be nude in our clothed society.

A first-grader at school seemed unusually aware of her own and other children's bodies. She wanted close looks at the other girls in the school lavatory, according to the tattling, and gleefully offered to pull her own panties down for the boys' amusement. In the classroom she often paraded around with her skirt pulled up to reveal her panties (something that is innocently done at three years of age, but not at six). Naturally, much giggling accompanied her "strip tease." When trying to divert the child's attention to a worthwhile activity did no good, the teacher told her firmly but kindly to put down her skirt and sit at her desk. One day the teacher asked the class why they giggled about the child's actions. They announced that "it makes me feel funny." "She looks dopey doing that." "I think she's dumb."

The teacher had a conference with the mother and was told that both parents made a habit of walking nude around the house. The nude adult bodies undoubtedly were too stimulating for this little girl. The parents had felt that their nudity and wholesome attitudes would teach their child respect for sex. They altered their ideas after hearing about her reaction away from home, and began to observe greater modesty and privacy within the family.

Correct vocabulary

Each body part and function has its proper name, and children should be taught to use it. If the child has heard the correct nouns from the beginning of his life, his vocabulary will contain many words by now which will aid him in asking questions and in understanding the answers. He should be able to use rightly such words as *navel*, *urinate*, and *bowel movement*. When a child wants to ask a parent about a specific part of his anatomy, and has not had occasion to use the name of it before, it is a good time to teach it to him; his need to know the word will make the teaching more meaningful. He may say, "Where my bowel movement comes out, it hurts." The parent can supply the unknown name, and by using it several times, the child is helped to remember.

The parent may say, "That opening is called the anus. Sometimes a bowel movement may cause a little irritation to the anus. I'll give you some vaseline to spread on your anus, and that should make it feel better." Later the parent may inquire of the child if his anus has stopped hurting. The word will soon be part of the young child's vocabulary.

Occasionally little children are curious to know the name of the place where urine comes out in a girl. They can see that the penis is used in a boy, and so wonder what it is called in a girl's body. The adult may answer by saying, "The urine leaves the body through a passage called a urethra. Everyone has a urethra. A urethra goes through the penis, also."

Knowing the correct names gives dignity to the conversation; it does not invite perverted humor, nor does it cause embarrassment to the speaker.

Children are curious about their navels. If a child has not been taught why he has one, it may cause him embarrassment. Asking another child if he has a "belly button" may make him look foolish to his friends and cause teasing. By this age he should use the word navel and know why he has one. If a child uses an incorrect term, the parent or teacher may say in a matter-of-fact way, "That's called a navel." His questions of why he has one and what purpose it has must be answered simply and honestly. "We call it a navel, because that is its real name. Every human being has a navel. Before you were born, when you were growing in your mother's uterus, you weren't old enough to eat or drink milk, there was a very special way for you to get nourishment. There was a cord attached to a special place in Mother's uterus, and the other end was attached to you. In a very wonderful way, Mother's body made nourishment that went through the cord to you. This special food made you grow bigger and stronger. When you had grown big enough and strong enough to live outside of your mother's body, you were born. After you were born, you could breathe and cry and drink milk, so you did not need the cord any longer. The doctor tied a thread (what he calls a suture) around the cord and then clipped it off. Your navel is a little scar showing where the cord was. That's how all people started life. That's why everyone has a navel."

Naturally the child's next question or statement will be, "I bet that hurt me when the doctor cut the cord." To this the adult may answer, "No. It doesn't hurt the baby or the mother when the cord is clipped."

As the child grows older, his understanding about new life and birth also grows; bits of information are repeated over and over by the adult and added to, as the child's ability to understand grows. It is impossible for a child to grasp the entire story at one time. Let his questions be the guide as to the time and amount of information he is ready to accept.

Buttocks is another word a child should add to his vocabulary. "Fanny," "can," "seater," "bottom," and such nicknames are not understood by all, and also encourage laughter. No part of the body should be scorned or laughed about.

A little child went running to his teacher and threw his arms around her. With tears flowing and between great sobs he cried, "Michael kicked me on my can!" The teacher had never heard the expression before, and was at a loss as to what part of his anatomy had been insulted. The children who gathered around found it a new word, too, or they would have furnished the information. When the hurt child gained control of himself, he showed the teacher where he had been kicked.

"Oh, those are your buttocks," she explained. "Tell me what happened that made Michael so angry that he did such an unpleasant thing to you," she added. Michael and the child whose dignity had been shaken were soon on friendly terms, with the teacher's help. Michael was helped to see that he was never to kick anyone, for there were better ways to settle arguments; the other child learned, among other things, the word buttocks.

A teacher should always use the proper names for body parts. In giving directions for a game, she may say, "Sit flat on your buttocks and place your legs straight ahead of you. . . ." In this way, children hear the word, and it soon becomes familiar to their ears, and they can use it when needed.

The first grade learns about the family

The first grade can continue with the study of the family which was started in kindergarten. Through discussion, the teacher soon learns the extent of the children's understanding of the family, and she can plan her approach from that point.

The teacher may have as her goal "to help the children learn and understand that the family is a basic social unit in our culture and serves to propagate man." Her approach will be planned to evoke the understanding of this concept.

"Let us find out what our mothers and fathers do that helps us and many other people," the teacher may say. "Let us write down all the things we can think of. Shall we start with mother?"

As the children tell about their mother's responsibilities, the teacher may wish to write their contributions on the blackboard.

"A mother has babies."

"A mother cooks food for her family."

"A mother buys food at the store."

"A mother gets clothes for her children to wear."

"A mother keeps her children's clothes clean."

"A mother loves her family."

"A mother helps her children when they get hurt."

The children's list will grow longer and longer. They may have difficulty in thinking of something Mother does that affects people outside their family, but with a bit of guidance they will remember that someone's mother helped with an election, another teaches a Sunday School class, and another sent food to a sick neighbor. There are also mothers who go to work every day. Through their discussion, children will discover that a mother has many responsibilities.

In the same way, a father's responsibilities can be discovered and written down. In one class where the children were discussing the father's role in the family, their first comment was that a father makes money. Upon questioning, the teacher soon discovered that the majority of her children pictured their fathers as going to the office or factory and spending their days making pennies, dimes, quarters, and other coins and paper bills. After all, Father had said many times that he worked to make money for his family.

The teacher suggested that each child interview his father that night to discover how he got the money for his family. The next day the children had many stories to tell. The various kinds of work were listed on the board. One child's father was a letter carrier, one was an insurance salesman, one a doctor, another a city worker, and one helped build houses. As their list grew longer and longer, the children were astounded to see the many kinds of occupations there were. They learned a bit about each kind of trade, business, and profession.

When the children had finished learning about Father, they understood that he earned money by giving his talents, services, or education to help other people live a better life. They learned that the money he earned was used to give his family the many things they needed. Children also told the many other ways Father helped his family and helped Mother.

As the children were talking about the father, one child offered, "A daddy loves his family and is good to them."

At this point a little boy blurted out, "My daddy doesn't love his family. He always gets drunk and hits everybody and makes my mommy cry." The children looked with disbelief at the child who told this sad story. There was nothing a teacher could say that would erase the horrible fact. But she did suggest to the little boy that perhaps his father had times when he did not feel well, and then went on to another's child contribution.

Even though the teacher could not help the boy who was unfortunate enough to have such a father, he at least was learning that all fathers were not like his own. Perhaps the family unit could help him learn that there were other ways for a man to live and meet his responsibilities. Having a chance to tell about his fears may also have helped him emotionally. It certainly aided the teacher in better understanding and guiding her young pupil.

The children also examined themselves and tried to discover their role in the family. "I make my own bed." "I hang up my pajamas so my mommy doesn't have to work so hard." "I mind Mommy and Daddy when they tell me to do something—" these were some of the contributions.

"Do you think learning to read and write in school is one of your responsibilities?" the teacher asked. This suggestion brought many more ideas. The children liked the thought that at six years of age they, too, had many responsibilities. On the overhead projector, the teacher showed the 3M Company's transparencies entitled *The Family.* Each picture stimulated the children's thinking and brought out many worthwhile ideas about the role and responsibilities of individuals within the family.

Books were made by the children and "My Family" written on the covers. Each child drew a picture of every member of his family. The teacher reproduced the children's dictated lists of responsibilities, which she gave them to paste under the appropriate picture. The books were read over and over by the children and then proudly taken home to be read aloud to the family.

During story time, the teacher chose books about the family and people in a family. The children searched their reading books and found stories that related to their family study. These stories were eagerly shared during the reading period.

Large chart pictures, *Beginning the Human Story: A New Baby in the Family,* were presented by the teacher. Each day the children would study several of the pictures and tell the stories they saw in them. The family pictures encouraged them to ask questions, which were answered by other children or the teacher.

The new baby, shown in the series of charts, once again brought babies to the children's attention. The teacher asked if any of them had ever heard stories about their babyhood. Again the contributions began.

"Have you changed in any way since you were a baby?" asked the teacher. The changes told about were marveled at. "I learned to walk"— "I learned to talk"— "I learned to understand other people"— "I grew bigger"— "I grew longer hair"— "I grew teeth"— were all suggested.

"My, what a lot of changes and growing up you have done in your lifetime! If I saw a picture of you when you were a baby, I imagine I would have a very difficult time recognizing that it was you."

"I'll bring you a picture of when I was a baby, so you can see how big I've grown since then," offered one little girl.

"What a good idea! Why don't all of you speak to your parents and see if you have a picture you can bring to school. Write your name on the back and then wrap it up so no one can see it. If you give it to me, I'll put all the baby pictures on the bulletin board. Then we can try to guess which picture is Bobby's baby picture and which is Lisa's. We'll all try to figure out which picture belongs to each child. Now remember, don't tell anyone which picture is yours," suggested the teacher.

Several mornings later, when the children arrived at school, they found all the pictures on the bulletin board. They crowded around, studying each one to determine whose baby picture it was. The growth and changes made in their six years of life were tremendous, they discovered.

Learning about animal babies

If the children did not have the experience of seeing newborn animals or a newborn baby during their kindergarten term, the first-grade teacher should try to arrange for such an opportunity. Springtime at a farm or zoo gives children a chance to see many baby animals and their parents. These experiences open the door to questions and further learning, if the teacher is alert to the opportunities they present.

One teacher took her children to a dairy farm to see the modern "milking parlor." The trip also included a walk through a large barn. One very heavy cow was lying on the floor of her stall. The children feared she was ill and asked one of the farm hands nearby what was wrong with her. "She's just fine," was his answer. "We're expecting her to drop her calf any minute now."

"Drop her calf?" asked one child.

"Where is her calf?" asked another.

"Why, her calf is growing inside of her. See how her side bulges out? That shows where the calf is. The calf should be born any time now. On the farm we say she 'drops' her calf," explained the farmer.

"Where will it come out?" asked the wide-eyed children.

"Right between her hind legs," said the farmer in a very matter-of-fact way. "See that big bull over there? That's the father."

The teacher couldn't budge the children. They stood about and pleaded with the cow to cooperate and have her baby while they were there. But the cow did not oblige them. The driver's threat that the school bus would leave without them was the only thing that tore them away from the cow's stall.

What a deluge of questions followed that trip! The teacher read *All about Eggs and How They Change into Animals* on their return to school. A picture in the book showing a cow with her unborn baby in the uterus, and the next picture showing the calf at her side, delighted the children. More books about animals and their babies were collected by the children and the teacher at the school library. Films about baby animals were shown and discussed. The children particularly liked the film, *Kittens: Birth and Growth.* This shows the actual birth of a kitten, the mother cat caring for her litter, the little kittens nursing, and the growth of the kittens to the age where they are ready to be given a new home.

In the discussion that followed the film, the teacher reviewed with the children the mother and baby animals they had been learning about through firsthand experience and through books and films. With her questions, she helped them discover the fact that all living animals come from living animals, and that each animal reproduces an animal like itself. Through this exposure to materials and experiences dealing with reproduction, some children began to wonder how the new life happened to be in the cat.

CHILD: *Where did that mother cat get that baby that came out of her?*

TEACHER: *It grew inside of the cat in a very special place called the uterus.*

CHILD: *How did it get in there?*

TEACHER: *Inside every female animal and female cat are some very tiny egg cells. They are so tiny that you would need a magnifying glass to see them. When the male cat places a cell, a sperm cell, from his body in the female's body, the sperm cell enters an egg cell, and a new kitten begins to grow. It grows and grows until it is big enough to live outside of the mother cat's body, and then it is born.*

Some children will understand the teacher's explanation, some will understand part of the story, and others will miss the entire description of what takes place. All children, however, will understand that the baby kitten was born and came from the mother cat's body.

Again, it cannot be assumed that, because children have learned that kittens grow in the mother cat's body and are born, they will realize that human reproduction happens in much the same way. An alert teacher will use every chance that presents itself to help children learn that human beings also start life from two cells meeting and becoming one and then growing into a baby within the mother's uterus. When a child announces the impending birth of a new child in his family, or the arrival of a new baby, it presents a good opportunity for the teacher to read aloud a book about a new baby, such as *We Want a Little Sister*. Giving the children an opportunity to study the pictures in the book and ask questions often gives the teacher a chance to further their understanding of human reproduction and growth.

Children learn best when they want to learn and when they are mature enough to understand. The teacher should plan that, during the months she has her class, she will teach about animal and human reproduction at times when the children indicate a desire or need to learn about it. It is not a study that should be taught as a separate unit, but should be integrated with the regular classwork. It becomes a part of science and social studies, reading and art, and the whole process of learning about the world we live in.

Chapter Six

The Seven-Year-Old
at Home

The seven-year-old child

The seven-year-old is losing the last traces of his baby-like appearance and behavior, and he is entering a new phase of growing. The egotism of six is fading and is being replaced by twinges of self-doubt and self-criticism.

Complaints are common at this age, and the child often feels that parents, teachers, or other children do not like him. He is jealous of younger siblings, feeling sure that everyone loves the baby most of all; he is jealous of older siblings, for he knows they have many more privileges than he and is sure he is not being treated fairly. He wants to prove to people and to himself that he is really growing up, and often sets his goals too high.

When he cannot perform or achieve as he feels he should, he may become very angry and impulsively throw or break things. When he is seen doing something he knows he should not do, he tries to save face by insisting that someone else started the whole thing. It is very difficult for him to accept blame.

Gross bodily outlets

A child of this age is anxious to please parents and teachers, but often does things adults find annoying. At the dinner table he tilts back his chair, and occasionally goes over backward with a dramatic crash. There is once again an upsurge in the number of times his glass is knocked over, drenching the table with milk. His neighbors at dinner complain of being kicked, as his restless feet constantly swing about. Eating with shoeless feet can make those kicks less effective and ward off much bickering.

The child's need to move his growing body tempts him to hang from every possible nook or molding he can reach, leaving finger smudges and occasionally damaged wood trim on moldings not strong enough to hold his swinging weight. Statuary, railings, low fences, and shrubbery become challenges to climb, slide on, sit on, or jump over. Some adult always seems to be saying to him, "Don't do that! Can't you just walk? Must you jump?"

At school, while the teacher is talking, he may have deaf ears. If he is listening, he often accents his attention with pencil tapping, pencil chewing, or by rubbing damp fingers across his desk with a bump, bump, bump. To sit still and erect is almost more than he can do. His head seems too heavy, and a frequent position for him is head on hand, with his elbow propped on the desk. His hands are always busy, and he feels compelled to touch everything. He walks down a hall or up the stairs dragging his hands along the walls. At school, the flag hanging in the classroom needs to be touched each time he is near it. As far as the children can reach, the flag soon gets a very weathered appearance. When a child is asked by the teacher to keep his hands off the flag, his expression is one of disbelief. He was really not aware that he was playing with the silky material.

If the class flag-bearer ever makes a mistake and allows the tip of the flag to touch the floor momentarily, these same children who wiped their dirty hands on it will insist that the flag must be burned immediately. No child is quite sure whence he derived this dramatic idea, but year after year teachers discover that children repeat it. They insist that this terrible disrespect for the flag of our country is so great that the only way to correct it is to burn the desecrated flag. Fortunately for the school budget, teachers are able to convince the children that the error is not intentional and that therefore the flag has not been insulted. They go on to explain to the children that there are times when a flag should be burned. When an old, worn-out flag must be retired it is never placed in the garbage, for this would be very disrespectful to the flag of our country. The right way to dipose of a worn-out flag is to burn it. This is important information for the sincere seven-year-old, who is deeply interested in the correct procedure for such things. His self-righteous behavior becomes all mixed up with his own thoughtless actions, but intentions are good!

Seven's fears

Parents are often concerned about new fears their child exhibits at this time. Ghosts, weird creatures, scary shadows, all suddenly disturb him. One little girl insisted that after she went to bed an ugly man with flapping coattails scooted down the long hall outside her bedroom door. This imaginary apparition was not laughed at by her parents, but they assured her that it was most likely a shadow. When the hall light was left burning brightly, she no longer saw the shadow. The light kept the eerie creature out of the hall and the child was content. Other fears disturbed her from time to time, but her parents were always able to help her meet and conquer them.

Little Carol found a lovely way to handle her fears. There was a beautiful picture of Jesus on the cover of her Sunday School story, and she decided to cut it out and mount it on colored construction paper. Every night she prayed to Jesus, asking him to watch over her; having the picture of Jesus near her in sleep gave added strength to her faith.

Another fear many children have is starting second grade. They have had enough school experience to realize, and have heard from other children, that some teachers may be crabby and raise their voices at you (a seven-year-old says a teacher yells, if she needs to scold a pupil). They often torment themselves before school opens in the fall with fears of getting a new, horrible teacher. One little girl prayed all summer long, asking God to put her in a certain teacher's room. She had heard that this teacher was good to the children and smiled most of the time. Most second-grade children learn to love their teacher, even the new one in spite of their school-opening fears.

Child-family relations

On the whole, the seven-year-old gets along well with Mother. He is easier to discipline, but does enjoy arguing with her about her requests or suggestions. A favorite treat is doing something alone with Mother, such as having lunch at a restaurant, taking a nature walk, or playing a game with her. A grandmother who has time to read a story or have a conversation with a child this age will soon be one of his favorite persons.

The family is becoming more important at this time,

and the child now sees it as a unit. To pack a lunch and have a picnic in the park or go to the zoo gives a nice feeling of belonging together. To have one family member missing can ruin the picnic for the seven-year-old child.

One snowy night a family planned to have a "togetherness party." It was decided that the seven-year-old daughter could stay up until nine o'clock, since it was Friday night, for she could sleep longer in the morning. The family played a favorite table game, and then they all enjoyed a family-type program on television. This was followed by refreshments of popcorn and orange juice poured over crushed ice, with a gay colored straw protruding. The family party was so thrilling to the little girl that it was agreed to do the same thing the next Friday night. Soon "family night," as it was named, was an established routine. The same procedure followed each Friday, even to the popcorn and orange juice poured over crushed ice, with a straw to use for sipping. The seven-year-old child likes repetition, particularly of enjoyed activities, and wants nothing changed. The tradition went on for years, and no family member missed "family night" except on rare occasions. The parents refused many adult parties, since Friday's family night became as important to them as to the child. They saw the good that resulted from being together. These parties were a leisurely and happy occasion, when everyone had time to listen to the other members of the family. Many family plans and decisions were developed and completed during family night.

The seven-year-old child's socializing

The seven-year-old child likes to have a "best friend." Occasionally the duo may become so important to each other that they exclude other children for fear they may interfere with their friendship. It is also quite normal for this age to have a strong boy-girl love affair, with the conviction that they will some day be married.

Group play at this age is still not well organized, but the children are learning to be more cooperative. Some are able to lose a game without being distressed, but they need to win some of the games to console themselves. Boys and girls can still play happily together, but the boys are beginning to find playing house with the girls less interesting. They may play school with the girls, but often break up the game with silliness.

Girls still enjoy playing house, school, library, postman, and store. Some children enjoy activities such as cataloguing their own book collection, making library cards for each, putting books into categories by subject matter, alphabetizing titles, stamping dates for "book due," and collecting fines for overdue books. Each time they want to read one of their own books, they go through the regular library procedure of checking out the book. The organizing of their private library is the important part of the play; it may turn out that the only readers will be their dolls and stuffed animals.

Seven is the age of collecting stones, bottle caps, cards, and other such items. These collections are precious to the children but may be very annoying to a neat mother.

The seven-year-old and sex

The child of seven seems less interested in sexual differences than in the role and characteristics of boys and girls. Some children may still become involved in mutual exploration, but it is less than at an earlier age.

Children often beg to have a new baby in the family. They become intensely interested if their mother is pregnant and want to learn all about the baby's growth. They are curious to know how big the baby is at various periods of prenatal growth, how it is fed, and why Mother goes to the doctor. Their questions are often endless at this time.

CHILD: *How do you know for sure that a baby is growing inside you, Mommy?*
MOTHER: *I can see that my body is getting larger as the baby gets bigger. I can feel the baby move sometimes.*
CHILD: *How does it feel inside you?*
MOTHER: *It feels as though the baby is moving its arms or legs. Next time I feel the baby move, if you're here, you may put your hand on my body. You may be able to feel its little movements.*

How exciting it is for the little child to feel the first faint signs of life of his little brother or sister!

The child may inquire how the unborn baby is nourished in this prenatal stage, if he has not asked previously. One child was questioning his mother about how the fetus ate. When she in turn asked him how he thought the baby was fed, she learned that what she suspected was true: the child thought the food she ate passed down into the baby's mouth.

MOTHER: *The little baby isn't old enough to eat food with his mouth. He stays snug and warm in his very own special place called a uterus and the food I eat doesn't go near him.*
CHILD: *What does he eat?*
MOTHER: *He doesn't eat, but he gets nourishment from my body through a very special tube called the umbilical cord.*
CHILD: *What goes through the tube?*
MOTHER: *I call it nourishment. It's like food, for it helps the baby grow.*
CHILD: *Does he like the food?*
MOTHER: *He doesn't know he is getting it. It doesn't go into his mouth. Come, I'll show you a picture of a baby and the umbilical cord. (If a picture is not available, the adult might draw a sketch of the umbilical cord.)*

Another question a child this age often asks is whether the mother has ever heard the baby (fetus) cry. A simple answer will satisfy, such as, "We never hear babies cry until they are born." At this age a child also enjoys learning about the growth of the fetus. He will often ask, "About how big do you suppose the baby is now?" By "big," he is usually referring to the baby's length and weight. Most pregnant mothers have a book which gives such details about the growth of the fetus and can keep themselves informed on the growth pattern from month to month.

The average seven-year-old child is satisfied to know that a baby starts from an egg cell in the mother and a sperm cell from the father. It is rare for them to ask for more information. When a child has heard remarks made by older children or adults about the mating process, he may then be more curious.

CHILD: How does the sperm from Daddy get to the egg inside of you?
MOTHER: Daddy puts it there.
CHILD: Next time Daddy puts it there, tell me, because I want to see him do it.
MOTHER: No. That's a very private time. We're always alone. Daddy loves me very much, and one of the ways we show that we love each other is by having babies.

If a child continues to ask for more information, he may be told, "The sperms pass through Father's penis and enter Mother's vagina, and then travel all the way up to the uterus where the egg is. When one sperm enters an egg, a baby starts to grow. It takes a mother and a father to have a baby."

These answers should be given simply and with dignity. To become dramatic and emphasize the great love that occurs between man and wife at this time puts too much emphasis upon it and would make the child feel that something is wrong about the whole procedure. If further questions are asked about the sperms and eggs, the parent could draw a sketch showing the vagina, uterus, and ovaries.

Children who have not had a previous experience of having a baby born in their family will ask questions concerning the birth and the reason why their pregnant mother goes to the hospital.

CHILD: *Why do you have to go to the hospital to have the baby born? Is it like being sick?*

MOTHER: *No, it isn't at all like being sick. I'm going to the hospital so a doctor and nurse can take care of the baby and me. Mothers should rest for a while after the baby is born, and the nurses will take care of our baby while I rest and sleep. The doctor is there to cut the umbilical cord and to examine our baby and see that he is well cared for.*

CHILD: *How does the baby get out of the uterus when it's born? Where does it come out?*

MOTHER: *A very wonderful thing happens. When the baby has grown so big that he fills up the whole uterus and there is no more room, he starts to push hard and move, because he gets tired of staying in one position. When he pushes, one end of the uterus slowly starts to open. When this happens, muscles start to press the uterus and the baby gets pushed through the opening and into the vagina, which also stretches bigger. Then the baby comes out into the world through the vagina opening, which is between my legs.*

Should the child ask to see the opening, his mother should firmly but kindly refuse his request, "No, I won't show you, but I'll draw a picture for you so you'll understand."

Children are always eager to talk about the sex of the child to be born. Girls usually hope the baby will be a girl, and boys prefer their own sex. Parents occasionally banter goodnaturedly about what they want. Fathers have been known to say, "It had better be a girl or I'll send it right back to the hospital." This humor may be understood by older children, but not by the literal-minded seven-year-old. The boy in the family may feel that girls are the preferred sex, or that boys are special if the parent expresses the wish for a boy. Children should always be made to feel secure in the knowledge that each sex is good and wanted. Sometimes the careless remark of a father or mother may be angrily told to the little one at a much later date, when he is quarreling with an older brother or sister. Hearing that he really was not the sex his parents wanted may prove damaging to him.

The father and mother roles

The father, in particular, should take advantage of the receptiveness of the seven-to-ten-year-old child and gain good rapport with him. Fishing, ball games, or a trip to Father's place of business are all special treats that give Father a chance to share his interests with his child.

It is a wise father who includes his children, particularly his sons, in his responsibilities as father of the family. Showing his children where he works and telling them what he does to earn the money he needs to care for his family, help children gain a good "father image." Through the years, children should learn about and appreciate the many things Father does for them and for others. They should know the pride he takes in his work and his belief in the necessity and importance of what he is doing in the business or professional world. The children must also understand that Father does his work well in order to earn enough money for his family's needs, and that he feels it is an important and useful part of his life to protect, feed, love, and care for his family. His contributions to his community and church add to his importance in the eyes of his family.

Contrast this attitude with that of the father who drags himself home from his daily work bathed in self-pity; angry that he must work and hating his "stupid job" and his boss. When he gives money to the family, he makes them feel that he begrudges them every cent. His children—sons particularly—learn that it must be a gruesome thing to be an adult, certainly nothing to look forward to.

A boy who has a loving father and one he can admire has an image and pattern set for him that makes his goal as a man and father well defined in his mind. Homosexuals, upon being questioned, often admit to having had a very ineffective father and one who ignored his son.

Mother's role and her contributions to the family are seen daily by her children. Her love and respect for her husband and for her children are deeply ingrained in their appraisal and respect of the "mother image." The dominating mother and wife also makes a deep impression on her children's attitudes toward the mother and woman role. The wife who belittles her husband's contributions and shows him no love cannot expect her children to gain respect or admiration for either parent's sexuality.

When divorce is thrust upon children, most of them have a difficult period adjusting to the usually unwanted situation. It is often better accepted by the children if parents do not shatter their images of mother and father. Knowing that their mother and father still love them and that this traumatic situation was not in any way their own fault helps to keep the involved children from feeling that their world and security has been pulled completely out from under them. When the parents' love for their children is constant and shown to them, the children usually manage to get through the change of divorce without too many scars.

The death of either parent brings its grief and problems to the children. In spite of the fact that the death can be shattering to children, they usually can weather it with less lasting damage than a divorce.

Animal reproduction

The children of yesteryear were seldom permitted to know that kittens or puppies came from their mother's body. When the babies were about to be born, the expectant mothers were carefully hidden away; the children were told that their pet must have run away, or that she was ill and must not be disturbed. The pet would then reappear a few days later with a litter that was miraculously "just there."

Fortunately, most of today's parents view this attitude as foolish. They want their children to be knowledgeable and alert about the world in which they live. Learning the amazing story of animal reproduction will add to their appreciation of life about them.

Although a parent wants his child to learn about reproduction, he often hesitates, for he is not sure how he should explain it to him. The safe way is to answer the child's question simply and truthfully. Answer only what the child has asked for. If he wants more information, he will ask for it. If he asks, he is old enough to understand. Pets and trips to the zoo, farm, or pet shop set the stage for such questions to be asked.

A dog in the family

When Susan and her parents moved from an apartment to a house, the promise of a dog went with it. Long before the move was made, research was started on dogs. Susan visited all her friends who had dogs. She asked each family dozens of questions about their pet. She brought home from the school library books that told about the many kinds of dogs. She read to her parents about the characteristics and sizes of the different breeds of dogs, and they would discuss and try to determine whether a certain breed would be suitable for their home

and their way of life. Finally, the field was narrowed
down to three kinds. Visits were then made to kennels
—and suddenly, there was their dog waiting to be
bought and taken home! It was a wiggly ball of scraggly
hair, with a tail that wagged wildly and an inquisitive
way of examining Susan's eyes and hair and ears. The
puppy completely captivated Susan and her parents.

With the dog held lovingly in the little girl's arms, the
trip home was used to review all the suggestions they
had read about how to make a dog happy in a new
home. The parents and the new dog owner also discussed all the dog-training ideas they had read about and
agreed upon. All decided that Susan's choice of Ange-
lique for the new pet's name was perfect, and that Angie
was a good nickname. Angie enthusiastically agreed to
their choice and showed her appreciation by thoroughly
licking Susan's surprised face.

The family helped their new pet to become a good
citizen. After several weeks, they agreed that their puppy
was unusually smart and was learning quickly the many
things they were teaching her. She was fast becoming a
member of the family, for she was a warm, happy friend
to have about.

When Angie was nearly two years old, the family felt
that such a fine, friendly dog should bring more such
dogs into the world. So once again research was done.
Care was taken to find a well-adjusted male as a mate
for Angie. The male dog and Angie agreed to the mating.

A book was read on the care of the pregnant dog and
what a family should do to prepare for the puppies. It
was a thrilling day when it was determined that Angie
was really pregnant. She received a special diet, vitamins, and plenty of exercise each day. Father made a
whelping box for Angie. Susan was responsible for encouraging Angie to accept it, and Mother took care that
Angie received her daily vitamins. Susan encouraged her

friends to play gently with her pet, so no harm could come to her babies.

Finally the time came when the puppies should be born. The dog's restless pacing and panting alerted the family to the imminence of birth. Susan stayed near Angie and kept reminding her to use her whelping box for the birth of her babies.

When Susan's bedtime arrived and the puppies still had not been born, she pleaded to stay up, for she wanted to watch the long-awaited birth. With her parents' promise that she would be wakened when the babies started to arrive, she went to bed. The parents were as excited as their daughter, and kept vigil next to the whelping box which Angie had decided to use.

Suddenly one puppy arrived in its little membrane sack. The mother reacted like a veteran and immediately took care of her six-ounce baby. Susan was hastily awakened to see the new life. As if to oblige, a second puppy arrived. The family sat in silence and awe as they watched the beginning of another new life. The mother dog once again went about the business of getting the second puppy started in this world. With her tongue and teeth she licked and tugged and tore off the membrane sack, and bit off the umbilical cord. The little puppy was rolled over, back and forth, as that busy tongue helped him start breathing. Only after the little ball of wet fur started to make small squeaking sounds did the mother rest a little as she awaited the next birth. The two little puppies that could neither see nor hear used their God-given instinct, and with their little legs working like flippers they swam over to their mother's nipples and started sucking.

Finally Susan could manage to speak after witnessing this amazing feat, and she whispered in an awed voice, "It's the most beautiful, wonderful thing I've ever seen. Oh, Angie, I love you! It's a miracle, that's what it is, a miracle! Your puppies are beautiful, beautiful!"

Susan had learned that to start a new life, the reproductive cells of the male and the female were needed to unite as one. She learned that because of internal fertilization the babies could grow in the warm, safe, special baby-growing place which is the mother's uterus. She experienced the thrill of watching those joyous, energetic little puppies grow and seeing the mother dog protect, feed, discipline, and play with her babies.

It is hard to believe that anyone ever felt that children should not experience what Susan had the privilege to understand and witness.

Chapter Seven

The Seven-Year-Old at School

Behavior at school

The teacher usually finds children of this age anxious to please her, and very loving. They like to stand next to their teacher and hold her hand for a few minutes. After the children become well acquainted with her, she can expect little notes on her desk or handed to her with the message, "I love you."

The child of seven is learning to play with his peers more harmoniously, but is still quick to anger when someone does not live up to his expectations. When a teacher sees a child rush up and start to hit a classmate, her questioning for the reason of the assault almost invariably is answered with, "It's his fault, he started it," and the child believes this reason fully exonerates him. He is quick to alibi and seldom admits that he could be at fault. He has standards of goodness, and he wants to live up to them, but is easily led astray. He feels, however, that all other people should live up to his code of what is right and good. If he feels something is not fair play, he will quickly complain that it is "not fair" or "a gyp"!

91

Just a year or two ago, the child had difficulty leaving a picture or written lesson at school, for he had to show it to mother that very day. Now his treasures seldom get home; the desire is still there, but the pictures and numbers and writing get crammed into a desk which has accumulated objects and papers of all descriptions, and they rarely find their way out again.

Some boys and girls are very fond of each other, and may kiss one another when they think they are alone. If this is detected by the other children, they will tattle to the teacher. It is usually best to ignore the love affair, for the tattling is enough of a suggestion that it is not the usual school behavior. If it continues, however, they can be told, "Kissing is a rather private way of showing someone that you respect and love them. It's usually a good idea to kiss at home and not in a school." When children come from a loving and demonstrative family, the desire to kiss a loving friend is certainly not wrong.

One of the regular problems that arises every now and then in second grade is that of having a boy pull up a girl's skirt. The offended lass usually stomps directly up to the teacher and tattles, with an audience of indignant girls around her, waiting to find out what terrible fate will befall the wicked boy. The wise teacher will ignore the "naughty" implications. She may calmly say, "I'll talk to Johnny and tell him he is not to pull your clothes. We certainly don't want any torn skirts." She may then speak to Johnny in the same manner. Normally this will take care of the "shocking episode" and help the children put it in the right perspective. This usually originates as a form of teasing.

Another annual problem is that of boys chasing girls. Each spring, as the weather gets warmer and as sure as flowers grow and birds began to migrate north, little girls indignantly tattle to the teacher that Johnny or Jimmy, or even a young herd of boys, chased Mary or Jane home from school. Behind the indignant expressions on the little girls' faces is also a glint of excitement and enjoyment. The chase is really a form of flirtation. The girls encourage the boys with their relentless bantering or their suggestions that they are afraid, and then the race begins. Sometimes in the excitement of the game caution is forgotten and some child gets hurt.

One little girl was chased home for several days in succession by a screaming, laughing group of boys who threatened to kiss her when they caught her. Each day she victoriously escaped into her home door just in time. One noon she was asked to walk a kindergarten child who lived next door to her to the small child's home. The five-year-old child slowed the race, and they were caught by a pack of excited boys. The two frightened girls found themselves in a situation which had grown out of control and were fortunately rescued by a neighbor lady. The next few days the girls chose a different route home, and the boys found other challenges to capture their attention.

When parents and teachers can understand the reasons behind such play, it is easier for them to approach the problem objectively instead of emotionally. The teacher has the advantage of discussing it with all her children; she helps them see the enjoyment of the game and the dangerous elements, and guides them in weighing the one against the other. This does not necessarily end the problem permanently, but it does call for a temporary truce and prevents it from gaining momentum.

Plant reproduction

Too many people take our amazing world for granted. The sun rises and sets, the seasons change, our stores compete with each other to have the greatest variety of foods to sell, and the average person accepts all this without question.

Teachers can guide children in gaining appreciation and wonder for all the richness with which we are endowed. The minerals in the earth that are ours for the taking, the oils and gases that we pump from underground and undersea, the abundance of fish and amazing creatures in our waters, the good soil that brings steady harvests to men, are but a few of the gifts and wonders of our world.

One second-grade teacher asked her children one day, "What would happen if no plant on earth ever reproduced another plant?" Her question was accepted with general boredom. Finally, one little voice piped out, "Do you mean what would happen if a tree never had a baby tree, and a flower never had a baby flower?"

"That's what I mean," nodded the teacher. "What would happen if no plant on earth ever again reproduced a baby plant?"

"You mean that if I ate the last carrot on earth," mused the same little questioner, "then there would never be any more carrots?"

"That's right," answered the teacher.

"Gosh, I'd like that!" laughed the little boy.

"Yeah, but if we ate up all the potatoes and there were never any more, I wouldn't like that!" said a shocked little girl.

Bit by bit the children discovered more and more favorite foods they would not have. "Golly, I bet we'd all die if we didn't have anything to eat," one child suggested in wonder.

"Huh! I'd just eat hamburgers all the time. They're my favorite anyway," answered another smugly.

"But there wouldn't be any hamburgers," retorted a child. "Hamburgers are meat, and meat comes from an animal, and the animals would die because they wouldn't have any food."

"Some animals eat other animals instead of plants,

so—" started a little boy, but he was not allowed to finish; all the children realized that there would not be any animals to eat if the plant-eating animals all died, and even the bugs and insects would die. This time the silence that followed this revelation was one of wide-eyed awe.

"You're right," commended the teacher. "How wonderful it is that plants do reproduce! Does anyone know how they reproduce?"

"Sure, seeds!" came the quick answer.

"Yes, seeds grow new plants, but why?" she prodded.

" 'Cause that's what seeds are for," answered a confident seven-year-old.

"But why do seeds reproduce?" the teacher urged. "Why don't rocks reproduce?"

Once more silence fell, and again an answer was not forthcoming.

"Lisa, will you please get that bag on our shelf and bring it here?" asked the teacher, pointing to a bag of lima beans. Holding up the cellophane bag for all to see, she asked, "What are these?"

"Beans!" all answered.

"What else?" probed the teacher.

"Seeds?"

"You're right," agreed the teacher. "Do you think they'll grow new plants? Why aren't they growing now? You said they're seeds," she added.

"You have to plant them. My grandfather plants seeds in the ground, and pretty flowers grow," offered a little girl.

"You've got to water them, too," another child added. "And put them where the sun will shine on them." The suggestions began to tumble in. "Let's plant them," they all urged eagerly.

"That's a good idea, but first let's find out why these seeds will grow new bean plants," suggested the teacher.

"My, they're so hard! They feel like little stones. If we put them in water for several hours, they'll be easier to open," she offered.

Several hours later the teacher gave each child a half-dozen beans to examine. "Open them carefully, like this," she said, as she carefully split the bean in half with her fingers. "Then look very carefully and see what you can find." Little heads were bent eagerly over the beans the children were attempting to open.

"I found out, I found it!" shouted one child. "There's a baby plant inside. I see a leaf and the stem. Look!"

Soon all the children found it. Some ran for magnifying lenses to be sure they saw everything just right.

"That little plant is called an embryo," explained the teacher. "That's the life in the seed. We can make that embryo start to grow, and then it will grow and grow into a new bean plant. But if we want it to grow, we must give it all the things it needs to grow."

"Let's plant some," the children urged eagerly.

"What a good idea!" said the teacher. "Shall we have some experiments to see if the seeds really need soil and water and sun to grow?"

"Yes!" they all agreed. "Let's plant some seeds in soil and give them water and sun," added a child.

"Fine! Here's a flowerpot, and we can get some soil out by the back fence. Shall we plant another seed in a flowerpot, and water it every day, but not let any sun reach it? We could put it in that dark cupboard," suggested the teacher.

"Let's put a seed in dirt and in the sun, but we won't give it any water. Then we'll find out if a seed'll grow without any water," offered a child.

"Let's put seeds in water and in the sun, but not give them any dirt," added another child.

"What good experiments these will be! Shall we get started with our planting?" asked the teacher. Soon all the seeds were planted in the various ways suggested.

The teacher suggested that the seeds in the glass of water would rot, but her suggestion was challenged by one child who said, "Let's try it. It would be an experiment to see if they really do rot."

"A good idea, Jim," agreed the teacher. "And I have another way to plant them for our experiment. Let's take these paper towels and roll them to fit into this glass. We can put some beans between the glass and the paper. Then we'll add water, but not on the beans. The paper towel will take up some of the water, and that will dampen the beans," the teacher explained.

The seeds planted in various ways were labeled and set in their proper places.

Each morning one little boy gathered all the bean plantings and placed them on the table at the front of the classroom. He would then hold up each plant and read the label to the children, "Bean seed with soil and sun, but no water. Still no plant growing," he would announce proudly.

After several weeks, the children were able to determine their experiment findings. "You were right, Mrs. Smith," the keeper of the flowerpots announced one morning. "The bean seeds in the water stink awful. They're rotten and we've got to throw them away."

Naturally, each child had to smell the rotten seeds and make horrible faces to show just how offensive they were.

The poor little bean in good soil that stood in a sunny window but was denied water continued to stay in its dry seed stage. "Water is sure important to a seed," announced a child. "It just can't do a thing about growing without water."

The beans in the glass that received moisture from the damp paper towel grew long roots which the children could see. The stem grew long, with leaves, flowers, and small beans forming. The children decided that it did very well, but the stem was weak. "It most likely needs all that good plant food in the soil. I wouldn't grow strong if I didn't have food," commented a class member.

"Look at the bean that didn't get any sun or light," pointed out a little girl. "It's got the longest stem of all."

"Yes, it is long," agreed the teacher. "Does it look strong? Can anyone figure out why it grew so tall?" she questioned.

"I know why," said the boy who put all the pots on the front table each day. "It grew tall because it was trying to reach the little bit of light that went through the crack at the top of the door."

"No wonder it's so tall," all the children agreed.

"The green leaves are awful pale, and the stem is sure wobbly," commented one observer. "That's because it didn't have hardly any light at all."

"The best of all is the bean in good soil that had water and sun. See how green it is!" a boy pointed out.

"It's strong, too, and the beans on it look better," another little scientist observed. "Now we know for sure what seeds need to grow new plants. Our experiment told us," he added proudly.

"There are other ways than seeds by which plants reproduce. Do you know any?" the children were asked next.

"My mommy breaks off a leaf from her African violet plant and puts it in water, and a new little plant grows on the stem of that leaf. Then she plants the tiny baby plant and it grows, and then we have a new African violet plant," offered one child.

"Do you suppose your mother would give us a leaf to plant?" asked the teacher.

Plants from kitchen windows and sunporches began to pour into the classroom. Each child told how to grow a baby from their home plant. Even a tuber was planted. A child brought a large potato to school and showed the eyes of the potato to the class.

"See these things on the potato? Those are eyes. If you plant 'em they'll grow," the child told the class.

The teacher brought a very large flowerpot filled with soil, and the children carefully cut the potato into several parts, taking care that each had several buds or eyes. The potato chunks were planted in the large flowerpot, watered, and put on the window sill where the sun could shine on it. Several months later, the plant that had grown so rapidly started to dry.

"Our potato plant is dying," they complained.

"Let's dig into the soil carefully and see if we can find anything," the teacher suggested. How thrilling it was, when they dug up many small potatoes!

The library was again searched and many books about seeds and plants were found and read avidly by the children. They took the books home to share with their parents. Many parents encouraged their children's interest and told of window sills being overcrowded with plants and experiments.

After the class plant study, the children looked at the beauty around them and the food in the stores with wiser and more appreciative eyes. They had learned how important, how wonderful plant reproduction is.

The school teaches animal reproduction

The study of animals is usually part of the science curriculum for small children. They learn to group animals in categories such as mammals, reptiles, and fowl. In learning about chickens and birds they learn special characteristics of this group. Fowl have feathers, they are warm-blooded, two-legged, and their babies hatch from eggs. The teacher today carries this study a step further by helping children learn why the new life grows in the egg.

The study of mammals includes the characteristics of this group. Mammals are warm-blooded, have hair on their bodies, their babies are born alive, the babies drink mother's milk, and they resemble their parents at birth. Today the child also learns how the babies are born alive, and that they grow in the mother's (or female's) body.

The teaching of sex is usually not a separate study, but a part of the regular study of animals, plants, and the family and community. Therefore it is involved in science, health, and social studies.

In talking to children about animals, the teacher may say, "Do you know that all living animals come from living animals? Has any factory ever been able to make a puppy or a mosquito?"

"I can buy a kitten at the pet store," a child may say.

Another child may suggest, "My female guppy had babies."

"Where did the pet store get kittens?" the teacher may ask the children. "Did the store get the kittens from a factory?"

"Kittens come from mother cats," a child who knows may answer.

Amphibious animals

One teacher started her study of animal reproduction each spring. At this time she would go to a country pond and collect some frog, toad, or salamander eggs (these may often be purchased at a science laboratory supply house). On bringing the eggs to the classroom, she would place the jars with the eggs on the front table with a sign saying, "Do you know what is in these jars?"

Not a child missed seeing the jars the minute he or she entered the room. It paid for these children to stay alert, for the teacher had so many interesting things to introduce to her children. As they crowded around the big table, peering intently at the contents of the jars, many children verbalized about what they saw.

"Hey, I see some seaweed."

"The water looks kind of dirty."

"Maybe we're going to put little fish in there."

"I see some dots and gooey stuff."

"I see some eggs. I've got a book about a frog, and frogs' eggs look like that."

The teacher was waiting to hear someone decide that there were eggs in the jars, and she said, "You're right, Jimmy, there are some frog eggs there. Do all the eggs look exactly alike?"

Once again all eyes searched the jars, and they discovered that one group of eggs were in a large clump while the other was in long strips, like a rope.

"I have some pictures of salamanders and frogs and toads," said the teacher. "If you sit in your seats, I'll put the pictures in the opaque projector, and then the pictures will be large enough for all to see," she explained.

The children saw pictures of several different kinds of salamanders. They saw pictures of toads and various kinds of frogs. One picture was of two frogs, the smaller frog clinging to the back of the larger frog. This was from the book, *Tree Frog*, by Paul McCutcheon Sears, illustrated by Barbara Latham.

"Are they mating?" asked one child who had learned about the meeting of male and female cells.

"Yes they are," answered the teacher. She continued to explain, "Every spring all the toads and frogs go to lakes or streams and meet there. Instinct makes them do this. Each male finds a female for his mate. While they are in this position, eggs are released from the female's body; at the same time, sperm cells come from the male's body and cover the eggs. One sperm cell enters one egg, another sperm cell enters another egg. Whenever a sperm cell and an egg join, a new toad begins to grow inside the egg."

"Are babies growing in our frog eggs?" asked one child.

"Won't the mother and father frogs miss their babies?" worried another.

"No, they won't miss their babies," the teacher assured the child. "Frogs and toads don't even know they are starting new life. After the eggs are fertilized, which is what we call eggs that have combined with a sperm, the parent frogs hop off in different directions. They may never see each other again, and they would not recognize their babies if they saw them."

The children could not wait to look at their frog eggs again to see if babies might be growing. The hand lenses were used for careful scrutiny of the eggs. The children learned that the frogs' eggs were in clumps and the toads' eggs in long strings. Some children were certain that they could see the beginning of life in the eggs.

"Let's draw a picture of our eggs in the jars, and then write a story about what we learned today. If the eggs are fertilized and babies grow, we can draw more pictures and write more stories about that and about the animals that come out of the eggs. We can use all the pictures and stories to make a little book about toads, frogs, and salamanders," the teacher suggested.

This met with enthusiastic approval, and the children hurried to start their books. Some children asked if they could trace the pictures of the salamanders and frogs and toads that had been projected on the large sheet of white paper by the opaque projector. When the outlined animals were crayoned and water, plants, and other background items added, the results made attractive pictures to put on bulletin boards and story charts.

As days passed, the children were delighted to see little wiggling curled animals develop in the eggs in two of the jars. The eggs in the third jar seemed to make no progress, in fact there seemed to be fewer and fewer eggs. On Monday morning, no eggs were in the jar.

"Someone must have stolen the eggs in the jar," a little boy announced angrily.

"Oh, I'm sure no one would steal our eggs," soothed the teacher. "They aren't in the jar—you're right—but what do you suppose might have happened to them?" she asked.

"I bet I know," said a sharp little lad. "I'll bet a sperm cell didn't get in the eggs, and so they weren't fertilized; so no new life began, and the eggs just rotted away."

"What good thinking!" the teacher said. "I think that is exactly what happened, and so those eggs deteriorated."

The embryos in the eggs were watched vigilantly by every child, and when the first small animal wriggled free of the egg, the larva was greeted heartily by a ring of beaming faces. Care was taken to keep the larvae's jars in good condition and to see that there were plenty of water plants; the larvae ate the slime off the leaves of the plants, their only food at this time. Distilled water was added whenever evaporation lowered the water level.

The children used their hand lenses to examine the gills of the larvae, and they learned from their reading that these gills took oxygen from the water.

Finally, just before the end of the school term, the little tadpoles were growing hind legs and then front legs, and their tails were slowly getting shorter. When several animals had completed the metamorphosis and had become frogs, they had lungs to breathe air, their gills had disappeared, their small mouths that scraped slime off plants had now grown large, with insect-catching tongues, while their new long legs could help them swim in water and hop on land.

The children had been reading many books about amphibians, and knew their animals now needed a different kind of food. Live insects had to be caught. Several times a day, two children at a time went into a sunny area of the playground and swished a finely meshed net over the grass. They soon learned the technique of catching dozens of minute insects, which they transferred to the jars. A glass lid was put on the jars during feeding time, so the insects could not escape. The little frogs, sitting on floating water plants, hungrily snatched the food. Soon a new terrarium was made of an old aquarium by the children. They put soil and plants in the terrarium, with an old soup bowl to serve as a pond.

Fish

When the children studied about fish and how most of them reproduce, they were aghast at the mortality rate. They learned that one female fish was able to grow thousands of eggs in her body, and that she would deposit these eggs into a quiet place in the water. They also learned that the male fish would swim over them, spreading sperm to fertilize the eggs. The children visualized thousands of baby fish swimming happily about.

"What would happen if a sudden wave came just as the sperm cells were leaving the male fish's body?" asked the teacher.

"They might float away on the wave," was the answer, "and then the eggs wouldn't be fertilized."

"And then—no babies!" said another child, dramatically throwing up her arms in a gesture of futility.

"That's right," agreed the teacher. "Can you think of other things that might happen to the eggs or the baby fish?"

"Bigger fish and turtles might eat them. Why, a big fish could gulp down all the eggs a fish laid," suggested a child.

"Do you think many of the fish grow up to be big fish?" was the next probing question.

"Not very many," nodded a little child, sadly.

"Would it be a good thing if every female fish laid thousands of eggs, and every egg hatched and grew into a big fish that would lay thousands more?" the teacher challenged. "What would happen to our rivers and lakes and oceans if they all grew up?"

"There wouldn't be room for them all. They would splash out all the water!" said the children, laughing as they visualized the result.

"Do you think it is good that each fish lays thousands of eggs? Is it a good thing that bigger fish eat some of the eggs and baby fish?" continued the teacher. The answers were many.

"Fish have to eat to grow."

"What other food would fish find?"

"If they couldn't find food they would die!"

"It's good there are so many, many eggs and little fish, or the bigger fish wouldn't find enough food."

"I'm glad there are fish, because I like to eat fish, too."

"I like to go fishing with my dad, and I like to catch big fish on my line."

The teacher then asked, "Elizabeth, you said your female guppy had babies. Did she lay eggs?"

"No, they weren't eggs, they were fish," answered Elizabeth. "Her little babies came right out a little opening by her tail."

"So all fish babies are not born the same way," the teacher pointed out.

More egg-laying animals

A few days later the children arrived at school to find a large, round metal object on the front table.

"What is it?" the children inquired of their teacher. "Try to guess," was the answer.

"I see a little round window."

"Here are some little holes on this side."

"There are some on this side, too."

"It's something electric, because here's a cord."

"Does it come apart?"

At this point, the teacher took the heavy lid off, revealing a platform with holes, and a thermometer on a stand.

"Please tell us," pleaded the children. "We can't guess."

"I knew you would find this puzzling. It's very different from anything we have ever had in our classroom," the teacher answered. "It is called an incubator." Her city children looked perplexed. "An incubator does what a mother hen does—it keeps eggs warm so babies can grow inside the eggs," she added.

The children knew! They were going to have the wonderful fun of having eggs hatch right in their classroom. They clapped their hands, jumped up and down, and squealed with delight.

That day the children and teacher had to adjust the temperature on the incubator so that the thermostat would keep the temperature between 102 and 103 degrees. They read the directions that were included with the incubator. When they were satisfied that they knew what to do, the children suggested that the next thing they had to do was get eggs.

"Let's go to the grocery store and buy some eggs," they suggested.

"We can go tomorrow during recess, and see if they have eggs we can buy," the teacher promised.

The grocery store was a block away from the school, and the teacher stopped in that afternoon to talk to the grocer.

"The eggs I sell are no good for your incubator," the grocer said. "They aren't fertile."

"I know that, but the children don't" answered the teacher.

The next day the class walked gaily to the store, only to be told that the eggs would not grow new chickens.

"Why don't you have the right kind of eggs?" asked a child.

"These eggs are from a chicken farm. That egg farmer has chickens to lay eggs for people to eat. He's not interested in hatching new chickens, so it isn't necessary for the eggs to be fertile," the grocer explained.

"When we eat these eggs, we aren't keeping a little baby from growing," theorized a child. "I like that. I'm glad that I'm not eating a tiny new life when I have bacon and eggs for breakfast."

"You should try to get some eggs from a farm," the grocer suggested kindly.

On returning to school, the children had many ideas about getting the eggs, but no one knew a farmer. Finally one little boy beamed and said, "I got it! Let's look in the yellow pages of the telephone book."

The telephone book revealed the names and phone numbers of several egg farms. With the teacher's help, several children called on the telephone. The first farm listened to the small child's inquiry and answered, "There isn't a rooster on the place! We haven't one fertilized egg." Upon reporting the bad news to the class, a child asked, "Is the fertilized chicken egg like the toads' eggs? Does it mean that a sperm cell is in the egg?" The teacher recognized the children's readiness and need to know how chickens reproduce.

TEACHER: *Yes, a new life will not grow until a sperm cell enters the egg.*
CHILD: *How can the sperm get through the hard shell?*
TEACHER: *That would be much too hard for the tiny, tiny sperm. It goes into the egg (or ovum) before that thick shell forms around it. Many egg cells are in a female's body, and when she matures the eggs start to grow. This is when the rooster's sperms unite with the eggs.*
CHILD: *How does he get them in the eggs?*
TEACHER: *Do you remember how the male frog clung*

to the back of the female frog when they mated? Well, a rooster clings on the hen's back, too. But he doesn't spread the sperms over the eggs as they are laid; instead he puts a small opening that is in his body, through which the sperms flow, next to a special little opening in the hen's body. Then the sperms travel up a special tube called an oviduct to where the eggs are. When they meet, a sperm will enter and unite with the egg (or ovum).

CHILD: That way the sperm won't get lost or washed away like the toad's sperms sometimes get washed away from the eggs.

TEACHER: That's right. It is a safer way to fertilize eggs. Now, we must think of some way to get fertilized eggs. Why don't all of you ask your parents this evening when you are all together. They might know someone who could sell us some fertile eggs.

The next day a child came victoriously to school with the news that his mother would drive him to the country after school. A farmer who was a friend of his parents said he had some fertile eggs, and would be happy to donate two dozen.

What an exciting event it was when the eggs were tenderly placed in the incubator! The children put a small X on one side of the eggs, and an O on the other side. The markings would help them when they needed to turn the eggs. A small dish of water was placed near the eggs, and then the teacher gently put the heavy lid in place.

The children reviewed the suggestions for caring for the eggs and wrote a schedule of the work to be done. The children signed up for their chance to turn the eggs and sprinkle them with water.

Books were read, and the children discovered in *Wait and See*, by Constantine Georgiou, pages that showed how the embryo developed in the egg. They asked to have the egg embryo picture put in the opaque projector and shown on paper so that they could trace it. The enlarged picture was crayoned and taped to their classroom door for other children to see. It hung under a sign that said, "Quiet, please—Egg Hatchery." Each picture in the book showed the development of the embryo on a specific day. As the children drew them, they were placed on the door so the other children could see how the embryos were progressing.

Children from other classrooms visited the room to see the incubator and were given a chance to view an egg held up to a high-intensity lamp. This process, they learned, was called candling eggs.

As the children marked off each day on their calendar, the excitement grew as they approached the twenty-first day. Finally the zero hour arrived, to the minute. There never was a more quiet day in that classroom. They tiptoed about the room, whispered to each other, and hardly dared breathe for fear they would miss the first "peep." They peeked through the tiny window and even learned to see through the little air holes on the side of the incubator. They were sure they saw cracks in some of the eggs.

At afternoon dismissal time they left the classroom reluctantly and sadly. "Won't our chicken eggs hatch?" they asked each other. The next morning the teacher met the children with her finger to her lips, suggesting silence. As they tiptoed into the room they were met with a chorus of chirping. The children stood still, almost shivering, drinking in that wonderful announcement. Before they ran pell-mell to the incubator to be first to see the new arrivals, the teacher quickly suggested that they all sit in their seats and then quiet turns could be taken to peek into that wonderful box.

When most of the chicks were hatched and strong enough to stand, the teacher transferred them to the brooding box the children had made of cardboard cartons, with an electric light for warmth. Knowing how new life was started, knowing the great care that must be taken to hatch the eggs, made the fluffy little chick each child was permitted to hold in his hand a miracle.

The children learned that, by instinct, the mother hen would sit on her eggs until they were hatched, and that she turned the eggs just as the children had done. "And she can't even make an X and O on the eggs, so as to know which eggs she turned," said a child in amazement.

The children were shown the film, *Mother Hen's Family*, from Coronet Films. After the viewing, they discussed what they had seen and learned. They also read a number of books which showed the setting hen and told how she cared for her eggs and chicks. Some of the parents further enriched their children's experiences by taking them to zoos, farms, and museums, where they could see hens on their nests and other hens caring for their newly hatched chicks.

Mammals reproduce

The teacher can ascertain quickly, through discussion with her children, whether they have had the experiences of learning about the reproduction of kittens, cows, and other animals as described in the preceding chapters of this book, involving kindergarten and first-grade children. If she discovers that they have had opportunities to learn about mammal reproduction, a shorter time may be spent on the study at this level. However, if the discussions reveal that the children have not had instruction in this area, she may wish to adapt the suggestions made for the younger children to the seven-year-old level.

Seeing the film, *Kittens' Birth and Growth*, by Bailey Films, will help children recall that mammals grow inside the mother animal in a special baby-growing place called the uterus. It is good to discuss with the children once more the fact that the babies are born alive and that baby mammals drink mother's milk. Many children need to review facts often to learn them well, and a few may have missed earlier information, due to poor listening habits or immaturity. Other facts that children should learn about mammals is that the babies resemble their parents at birth, that they have hair on their bodies, and that they are warm-blooded animals.

The seven-year-old child may ask how the kitten eggs are fertilized.

TEACHER: Where do the kittens grow before they are born?
CHILD: Inside the mother's body.
TEACHER: What part of the body?
CHILD: In the baby-growing place. It's called a uterus, I think.
TEACHER: You are right. All mammal babies grow inside of the uterus. So where do you suppose the eggs are when they are fertilized?
CHILD: Inside the mother cat?
TEACHER: That's right. How do the sperms get to the eggs, so new kittens can grow?
CHILD: I know, the father puts them in through that special opening.

After learning about the precarious existence of the frog and toad egg babies, and the risk of chicken eggs being broken, not turned properly, or not kept at an even temperature during incubation, the children can readily see that the mammal's method of reproduction is far safer. They usually express great pleasure in learning that higher forms of animals and human beings have a better way of reproducing.

Extinct animals

Most seven-year-old children are intrigued with the dinosaur age. These gigantic creatures capture their imagination, and they often dream that they will some day discover one that is still living and has been overlooked.

Little John announced in class one day, after he had learned what "extinct" animals meant, "I'm going to faraway countries and find a big dinosaur. Maybe it'll be a female dinosaur and she'll have babies, and then we can have a bunch of dinosaurs!"

Quickly Ann spoke up and shattered his dream, "You know that's silly. To have new dinosaurs you'd have to have a female and a male."

To save a bit of John's dream the teacher suggested, "John, why don't you write a story about finding a dinosaur? Maybe you could find a male and female, and then tell what you did with them. Wouldn't they be fabulous pets?"

"Why did dinosaurs have to die, anyway?" asked Ann. "They sure were strong enough."

"What a good question, Ann! I have some books that tell about dinosaurs, and they tell what happened to them. Would you like to read some of the books and find the answer to your question? Then will you tell the class what you found out about dinosaurs becoming extinct?" offered the teacher. Ann enjoyed discovering the answer and sharing the information with her classmates. The books were eagerly passed from child to child, so that they could all learn more about these fairy-story-like animals.

The importance of an egg

"Let's make a list of all the animals we know that start life as an egg," suggested the teacher one day.

"Chicken," called a child. "Birds," offered another. The contributions came faster than the teacher could write them on the blackboard. "Ducks, fish, toads, frogs, turkeys, salamanders, turtles, snakes, moths, caterpillars," the children called out.

Finally there was a pause, and the teacher asked, "Aren't you going to mention kittens?" After a surprised pause, one child said, "Hey, that's right! The sperm cell enters the egg cell and new life starts. Kittens start from an egg, too!"

"Good, Tommy! You figured that out very well," praised the teacher. "All animals on earth start life as an egg."

Human beings

"Who can show us on the blackboard the size of the frog eggs we had?" the teacher asked her children. After the small circle was drawn, she asked, "Now, who can show us the size of the chicken egg?" Several other animal eggs were suggested and also drawn.

The teacher then went to the blackboard and made a very small dot. "That little dot is bigger than the egg you started from. Isn't that surprising? You, too, started life as an egg. Do you know where that egg was?"

CHILD: *In my mommy.*
TEACHER: *Where in your mother?*
CHILD: *In her stomach.*
CLASS: *Not her stomach. It would have been digested!*
TEACHER: *That's right. The egg came from the place where only eggs grow. There are two of these egg-growing places, and they are called ovaries. The eggs are also called ova, and the places where they grow are the ovaries. You didn't start to grow in the ovaries, however. Do you know the name of the place where you grew?*
CHILD: *Uterus?*
TEACHER: *That's right, the uterus. Some people call it a womb. Can you remember the name uterus?*
CLASS: *Uterus.*
TEACHER: *Good for you. Uterus is the name for the very special baby-growing place inside each mother.*

Oftentimes this is enough for a child to understand at one time. More information can come later. It will surely be referred to again by the children, for they are learning that they can ask their teacher questions about things they want to know. The teacher may continue the study by helping the children learn about the differences and similarities of the human being and other mammals. Through her directed questioning they learn that human beings, too, are born live, resemble their parents at birth, drink mother's milk, are cared for by their mothers when they are small babies, have hair on their bodies, and so are mammals.

"Now, let's discover the ways in which we as human beings are different from other mammals," a teacher asked her seven-year-old children.

"Our daddies earn money."

"We live in a house."

"We go to school."

"We eat our food at a table."

"Our mommies cook our food."

"We go on vacations in our car."

"We have a better brain."

The teacher quickly answered the child who mentioned the brain. "You're right, David. We human beings have a far better brain than other mammals, and that is why our lives are more interesting and we are able to do so many things other mammals can't do."

"Wouldn't it be crazy if a cow drove a car down the street?" laughed Tony. Naturally, children loved the thought of an animal performing like a human being, and many more suggestions were made.

"Wouldn't it be fun to use our imaginations, and write some funny stories about animals that acted like human beings?" the teacher suggested, being aware that children have very creative and active minds. "I have a book about this very idea, which I will read to you during story time. It is about an elephant that acts like a human being."

"The brains we have," continued the teacher, "make

it possible for us to live on a much higher level than animals. We human beings are very precious and can live a good life. We can control and use other animals to make our lives better. Can you think of some ways that we use animals?"

"We eat the hen's eggs."

"We eat meat."

"We have animals for pets."

"The birds sing for us."

"They eat mosquitos, too, and I don't like mosquitos."

"We like animals in our zoo."

"My mommy has a fur coat."

"My shoes are made of leather."

The children enjoy learning that they are the superior animal. Often this is their first examination of their own and other human beings' many abilities and talents. They can discover the innumerable ways in which our lives differ from those of animals; among other things, human beings have the ability to plan, reason, choose, and chart their futures, and they have feelings of responsibility for their actions, and a conscience. Children like to discuss their own responsibilities and the responsibilities of parents, teachers, and other people with whom they have contact.

When babies grow

Oftentimes children will open the subject of human reproduction. An alert teacher can use the situation to make it a class learning experience. For example, one class was having a "show and tell" time, and little Mary announced, "My mommy is pregnant, and she's going to have a baby in three months."

"How do you know she is, and why doesn't she get it now?" challenged Bill.

"Mommy said the baby isn't ready to be born now, but we'll have our baby in three months. And my mommy is pregnant!" answered Mary firmly.

"What wonderful news, Mary," interjected the teacher. "What does it mean for a mother to be pregnant?"

"It means a baby is growing," shouted several children.

"And where is the baby growing?" questioned the teacher further.

"In the uterus," came the answer.

"How well you remember! Mary, do you know how long it takes for a human baby to grow?"

"Nine months, and our baby will be born in three months."

"A human baby takes much longer to grow than a baby chicken. Who remembers how long it took the chicken eggs to hatch?" the teacher asked.

"Three weeks," came the reply. "And a puppy takes two months," added Tommy.

"Who remembers how all animals start to grow?" the teacher asked.

Once again the children reviewed the facts that all animals begin life as an egg and that the egg must be united with a sperm.

Some children, even though they are seven years old, may still be very hazy about how a baby grows in the uterus. They will want to know that it receives nourishment and air through the umbilical cord, which is attached at one end to the mother and the other end to the baby; that the navel is the little scar that is left, showing where the umbilical cord was attached to the baby. Children find it very interesting to learn that the baby floats in a liquid, called the amniotic fluid, which keeps it safe from jolting; and that the temperature in the uterus stays constant, even though the mother walks from her warm home into zero weather. Children are delighted to learn how wonderfully comfortable and safe the developing baby is in the mother's uterus.

Mary's mother was invited by the teacher to visit school several weeks before the baby was to be born. The mother entered the room in the same manner as all visitors and asked if she might visit Mary's classroom for a while. The children stared openly, for here was that special mother who would have her baby very soon. Several little children passed her as she sat in the visitor's chair, and soon began to ask her questions.

"Can you feel your baby in your uterus?" one child asked.

"Can you feel the umbilical cord?"

"Is the baby heavy?" And question after question followed. Mary's mother was gracious, not at all self-conscious about her pregnancy or upset by the curious children; she answered the little ones' questions easily. She also promised to let the children see the baby after it was born.

One morning Mary came to school beaming and said she had an important announcement to make. She stood in front of the class and said, "My daddy telephoned this morning, and he had a smile from here to here," said Mary, drawing the smile with her finger on her face to show the bigness of the smile. "He said, 'It's a girl!' "

The class broke out in spontaneous clapping, their faces beaming almost as brilliantly as Mary's. Not one child questioned Mary how she could see her father's smile on the telephone. They all knew what she meant. Three weeks later Mary announced that her mother was bringing the baby as she had promised, that very afternoon. The teacher asked Mary if there were any rules about new babies and their care that the children in the class should know before the baby arrived.

"I can only touch the baby after I wash my hands. I speak quietly to her; if I yelled, the loud noise would frighten her. My mother keeps everything in her crib very clean," Mary enumerated.

"Thank you, Mary," the teacher said. "Now, children, how shall we prepare for the new baby? Where can Mary's mother put the baby so we can all see her?"

"I know," said Bill. "On your desk, because it's high, and then we can all see her."

"But first we must take everything off the desk and scrub it clean," suggested Beth.

"Can we touch the baby?" asked James.

"Do you think it would be a good idea if everyone touched a brand new baby?" the teacher asked. She received the answers she hoped for: the children decided that every precaution should be taken to avoid disturbing the baby; they should not risk frightening her by so many touching hands, and also the possibility of germs reaching her from so many mouths and hands close to her was too great. So the children agreed that they should stay in their own chairs and sit very quietly.

Several children scrubbed the teacher's desk top, the children's chairs were placed so all could see, and everything was in readiness when mother and baby arrived.

Mary hurriedly washed her hands and went out into the hall to greet her mother. This very sensitive mother understood Mary's thrill and pride in showing her wonderful baby sister to her friends, and so she put the precious bundle in Mary's arms. When Mary entered the room with her sister, a small gasp of wonder came from each child as he felt the awe and the impact of this special moment. After Mary handed the baby back to her mother to be placed on the desk, the mother unfolded the blanket and let the children see the very small infant.

"See her tiny hands? See how wee her little feet are," said the mother as she held the hand and then the foot up for them to see.

"Baby Lynn mostly sleeps and eats and cries," she

went on. "There are only a very few things she can do, so we must take care of her all day and all night. All she can do is sleep, suck her milk, cry, wet her diapers, and hold on to my fingers with her little hands. Her little fists can hold on quite well. Let me show you." With that she put her fingers up to the baby's hands, and when the baby had a good grip she pulled the baby's shoulders a few inches off the desk.

"Now let me show you something else, and watch very carefully." With that the mother held the baby in a reclining position, and waved her hand in front of the baby's face. Then she waved her hand in front of Mary's face. "Did you notice anything different between baby Lynn and Mary?" the mother asked.

No one could answer, and so the mother repeated the gesture several times. Children's hands shot up.

"Now you saw it. Jimmy, tell me the difference," Mary's mother said.

"Mary blinked, and Lynn didn't," was Jimmy's answer.

"Right! Can you guess why?"

"The baby's blind!" answered one child in a shocked voice.

"No, Lynn isn't blind, but her eyes need to grow and develop more before she can see everything the way you do. When they are first born, babies can only see lights and shadowy objects, but as they grow their eyes get better and better. Can you think of anything else that still has to grow?" the mother asked.

"Her teeth."

"Her hair."

"She has to grow bigger."

"She has to grow stronger."

"So she can walk."

"She has to learn to talk."

"And read!"

"My, how many things Lynn must do and learn before she gets as big as you," said the mother with a big smile for her delighted audience.

After the visit, the teacher was asked many, many questions. Once again the often-asked question came, "Where did the baby come out?"

"Through a very special birth canal called the vagina," answered the teacher. "When a baby is ready to be born, the vagina stretches like rubber, so the baby can come out into the world. When a baby is not being born, the vagina is very small."

Answering questions

The next day the teacher announced that she had some pictures to show about two babies. She placed the first transparency of *Characteristics of Boys and Girls*, published by 3M Company, Education Services, on the overhead projector. It is a picture of two newly born babies, wrapped securely in blankets, at which an older child is looking admiringly.

The children studied the picture for a few seconds, and then the questions began.

CHILD: *Are they twins?*

TEACHER: *Yes, they're twins. They're the same age. Their brother likes them. Doesn't he look proud!*

CHILD: *Are they girls?*

TEACHER: *I don't know.*

CHILD: *Are they boys?*

TEACHER: *I don't know.*

CHILD: *I think that baby is a girl (pointing to child at the left).*

TEACHER: *What makes you think it's a girl?*

CHILD: *I don't know; I guess she looks like a girl.*

TEACHER: *Who would know?*

CHILD: *The mother and the daddy.*

TEACHER: *How would they know?*

CHILD: *Well, a boy has a penis.*

Sometimes children look startled when they hear the word penis said aloud in a classroom. The teacher's dignity gives dignity to the situation. She may say, "Yes, doctors and parents have only one way to tell whether the infant is a boy or girl, and that is whether it has a penis. If the baby does have a penis, he is a boy; if not, the baby is a girl."

If there are a few rather silly glances or giggles among the children, they can be easily controlled. The teacher may say, "I know that some words we are saying are the kind of words we don't use in public. They are family words. If we want to learn about ourselves and nature we must use the correct vocabulary in class. We don't use these words when we talk on the playground or in a store. I think everyone in this room is old enough to understand the difference. If there is someone who feels he isn't old enough to use scientific words in class, he may leave the room and go to the library or to the learning center." Needless to say, all the children want to prove that they are mature enough to discuss things in a scientific way, and the silliness is quickly dispelled.

The series of transparencies continues through to the twins' double wedding. The final transparency shows the man twin and his wife admiring their baby, for they become a father and mother. The children enjoy the series of pictures, and fine discussion results from their showing. A teacher can choose which pictures to show her class, depending upon the maturity and background of her children.

There have been more and more books and visual aids reaching the market during the last few years, which are helpful to the teacher in guiding her children to an appreciation of the stream of life in this amazing world of ours.

Chapter Eight

The Eight-Year-Old
at Home and School

Behavior at eight

The eight-year-old is beginning to look more mature. His play is more boisterous, and he seems to thrive on rough-and-tumble type games. A boy, in particular, usually does everything in high gear. He has no time to tie his shoes, pull up his socks, keep his shirt tucked in, or comb his hair. He bolts down his food and then asks to be excused to race off to something more important. If told to stay at the table, he may treat the family to loud belches, followed with an automatic, "I'm sorry." He often points out that he feels bloated. When an important guest is at the dinner table, or if the family is eating away from home, the eight-year-old may suddenly be a model of decorum.

At this age the child wants adults to treat him like an adult. His need to have people realize that he is maturing is great. For parents to keep him on the same level as a younger sibling is wrong. He should have some extra privileges that come with his greater age, such as a slightly later bedtime, or the right to travel farther away from home base than a six-year-old brother.

Most children at this age still love Mother best, but Father is becoming increasingly important and is receiving more of the child's affection. Some children demand much attention from their mothers. They actively seek a closer relationship with her; they insist they are to sit next to her in the car, that it is their turn to play a game with Mother, that they have something important to talk over with her, and that they planned to bake cookies with her. Some mothers complain that their eight-year-old child will even invent an imaginary headache or stomachache to try to keep her from leaving the home for a social event.

In spite of this great show of affection for Mother, the eight-year-old may become extremely angry with her and call her "names." Even though he may be furious with her, he usually controls himself and will not physically strike his mother; but he may give a clout to a younger sibling who has the misfortune to be near by during a siege of temper.

The eight-year-old child resents direct orders and wants his parents to give him hints to correct his behavior. Firm rules and standards of behavior must be set for him, but he cannot accept calmly being reminded of them repeatedly. He will often respond to more subtle suggestions, such as posting a written list of duties on a bulletin board, or saying, "You won't be ready for your favorite TV program, if you don't attack that messy room of yours soon." He can accept the veiled threat of being denied a TV program better than the rough approach of, "Get in that sloppy room of yours, and don't come out until you've put everything in its place."

Household tasks that were happily performed at a younger age are now resented. If parents suggest a new list of chores, they are often accepted without complaint. A boy usually enjoys tasks such as repair jobs, especially if they entail what he considers a more adult approach. Fixing a broken electrical socket, being in charge of the trash, or nailing a loose board in place seem more challenging than drying dishes.

Girls often wash the dishes happily, but complain bitterly about drying them. Being responsible for a part of dinner preparation can be performed by some children. One eight-year-old girl was in charge of making the coffee each day. She measured water and coffee more accurately than most adults would do, and carefully timed the moment to start the coffee so that it would arrive at the table at just the proper time. The praise of the adults for her coffee made the duty one she jealously guarded.

Peer groups

Boys and girls of this age often segregate themselves in play, yet enjoy being together for certain games in gym classes or on the school playground. Mixed birthday parties, however, usually end in chaos and tears. A group of boys may shout at a group of girls, causing much loud, abusive noise. Girls, too, often band together to taunt the boys. A few minutes later the two groups may combine happily for a different type of play.

In group play, which the eight-year-old dearly loves, there is much arguing and anger, but the play goes on. The children's frank criticism of one another brings about group discipline and helps to keep the game intact. If one child feels offended and quits the game, the group's jeers soon teach him that such behavior is not fitting at eight. The child who is not telling the truth is quickly told, in shocked voices, that he is a liar. The group's ruthless scoffing at the lie is more effective in breaking the child's bad habit of fabricating than parents' carefully planned approach to the problem.

A child who is severely criticized by the group for his poor behavior, or reprimanded by parent or teacher for a misdemeanor, may take time out to pout and lick his wounds, but soon will actively try to make up. He is even able to admit he has done wrong, but tries to give reasons why it is not all his fault and why he should not be too harshly criticized. It is important to him to try to prove that the other person started a fight or wrongdoing.

The eight-year-old and sex

Sex differences beween boys and girls are becoming more noticeable at this time. Some girls choose only their own sex for friends and often express their opinion that "boys are dumb." A goodly number of children, however, still are interested in boy-girl relationships, and a few "engagements" continue intact from age seven. A boy may announce that a certain child is his girl friend and that she is pretty, but resents being teased about her. There are girls who like to chase boys they think are cute. One mother of a third-grade girl, trying to advise her daughter that it was unbecoming to be the pursuer, was nonplussed by her child's happy reply, "But Mommy, this is the age of open pursuit! Let me enjoy it!"

There are usually a few children who may still experiment with sex, both homosexual and heterosexual. These children often find the play disturbing, feel pangs of guilt, and usually end up disliking each other intensely. If a mother or father discovers that his child is or has experimented, angry scolding will simply add to an already burdened conscience. It is more helpful to talk to the child calmly and with understanding.

MOTHER: *Don't you feel you are too old for that sort of play?*
CHILD: *I hate her!*
MOTHER: *I'm sure you're angry with her. I imagine you are angry with yourself, too.*

CHILD: *Well, really it was her fault. She made me do it.*

MOTHER: *Are you sure that she made you do it? Sometimes people ask us to do something we feel is not good, but we don't know how to tell them we won't do it.*

CHILD: *Well, that's kinda like it was. I really didn't want to play that way.*

MOTHER: *I'm sure you hadn't meant to play in that way. You will have to learn to say, "No, I won't do that. I'm much too old to play such games."*

CHILD: *But what if someone won't listen?*

MOTHER: *Then you'll need to be very strong and not allow anyone to make you do something that is foolish or babyish, or not good. Just walk away, and find someone else to join. You can always come to me and we'll talk about it.*

If the eight-year-old tends to play with older children, it is necessary that the parents observe the relationship carefully. An older boy or girl may choose a younger child for a friend with the desire of indulging in sexual play, something at which his own age group would undoubtedly scoff. This older child may choose either his own or the opposite sex for this sexual stimulation. Parents should alert their child to the possibility of coming in contact with this type of maladjusted youngster and help him to know how to handle it. If parents can talk freely to their child about such experiences as these, the child will be encouraged to confide in them if he is ever accosted with such a suggestion. This warning should not create fear in him, but be offered to help him know how to react to and handle such a situation.

Some eight-year-old girls enjoy rolling around the floor in a play-type wrestling match with a boy. If a parent observes that this contact causes the girl to have "gooseflesh" or other signs of sexual stimulation, the girl needs closer supervision than most girls her age. She may be a child that can easily be drawn into group sex play with older children. She should be told firmly that such play is babyish and unbecoming to a girl her age. Through subsequent parent-daughter discussions, the child can learn the need to respect her own body, and that it is necessary for her to keep others from touching her body in a too-familiar manner.

All children must be cognizant of the perverted sexual adult who may contact them at some time. Teaching a child to play in open areas, stay out of alleys and apartment basements, never talk to strangers or accept their bribes, is as important as teaching him other safety rules.

One eight-year-old girl who had been thoroughly warned by parents and teachers was nonetheless drawn into a frightening experience. A well-dressed young man started to talk to her and her friend as they were jumping rope on the front sidewalk. He told them that he was a friend of their parents and that he lived in their apartment building. He was completely charming to the girls, and after a friendly conversation invited them to go with him to his apartment. He told them that he had some beautiful paintboxes he would give them, for he no longer needed them himself. The girls went willingly with him to an apartment which had just been vacated a few hours before (unbeknownst to them), for the tenants had moved out. When the girls discovered the apartment was empty, and that the man carefully bolted the door upon entering, they became frightened. He suggested that they take off their dresses, which the shocked girls firmly refused to do. He then removed his trousers, exposing himself to them. At this point they both started to scream and run through the rooms. He caught one child, but the other got away, screaming lustily. This child managed to dodge around the rooms and finally unlocked and opened the back door. The man could not hold one struggling child, suppress her screams, catch the second child, and guard both doors. The frightened screams went out the open back door, at which point the man hastily released the one girl, put on his trousers, and slipped out the front door. He was never apprehended, but fortunately the girls' screams and courage kept them from bodily harm.

Later the girls explained to parents and police that they thought bad men were ugly to look at and were strangers. They had believed the man's lies that he was a family friend and said he looked just as a regular father would look.

Many parents are torn between their desire to warn children of the sexual pervert and their fear of causing their child to associate something ugly with sex. When warning children about such men and women, it is not necessary to mention sex to them. Telling the children that these strange individuals are mentally ill and that they want to kidnap or hurt them is frightening enough to children to have them heed your warnings.

The experience of the two little girls underlines the need to be very explicit in helping a child understand who is a stranger, and that these people will lie to try to deceive and persuade a child to go with them. Reassure children that they will be safe from such fiends, if they follow your rules.

Masturbation

Parents are often disappointed to find that their child is still, or again, masturbating. Most children will occasionally handle their genitals. This may happen because the child feels the need to urinate, but does not take the time to relieve his bladder. Infrequent masturbating may be ignored by the parent, or he may say good-naturedly, "Please, won't you take time to go to the toilet. Let's not have an accident at your age." Normally this is accepted as a joke by a child, but also hints that he really should not be handling himself in such a manner.

Teachers also occasionally find a child contentedly masturbating, while sitting at his desk intent on reading or daydreaming. She can speak to him privately and suggest that he may wish to go to the lavatory. Often the startled child will say, "I don't have to go." The teacher's friendly reply, "Oh, I'm sorry, you looked as though the need were urgent," suggests to the child that his actions are not normal classroom manners, yet does not embarrass him. These small hints help the child who only indulges in such manipulation occasionally.

If an eight-year-old actively masturbates a great deal, it would be wise for parents to try to determine if their child is having some problems of which they have not been aware. Masturbation is not the cause of the problem, but often a symptom of some emotional or physical disturbance. Is the child secure and happy with his own peer group? Does he perhaps fear that his mother and father are not happy and may separate? Could he have a physical problem, such as a urinary infection or irritation of the skin?

Oftentimes an abundance of parental attention and love will help the child. Knowing that his mother and father are happy with him even though he has not been an outstanding student at school, or that they are not disappointed that he is not as athletic as Tom next door, makes the comforting self-love of masturbation unnecessary.

Most important of all, a child should never be made to feel ashamed or guilty of wrongdoing, if caught handling himself. Threats, fears, anger, are all ingredients of making a bad habit loom much larger and more important than it really is. The habit in no way harms a child physically; it is merely a habit which should be cast aside as the child grows older and becomes more interested in others.

Boys and the new baby

Some boys of eight seem to have been deaf and blind to all previous exposure given them about how parents get their new baby. Their past lack of interest is perhaps the reason they were so unreceptive to the information given them. In contrast, other boys appear to know all they want or need to know at this age.

The boys who are just awakening to the fact that there is much they do not know will begin to search. Hopefully, they have good rapport with their parents and will go to them with their questions. If the parent cannot or will not supply the answers, their child will undoubtedly ask his peers.

Parents should always keep tuned in to their children. The parent with a loquacious child sometimes finds this difficult. He allows the child to prattle on and on while he has his own ears closed to the chatter, and his attention is given to his own thoughts. This child's questions may be easily overlooked.

The boy of eight who appears interested, but does not question his parents about babies, may need a bit of prompting by an adult. Normally parents who have an eight-year-old child have friends of their own age group, and one of these undoubtedly will have or expect a baby. Telling the child about the happy event often leads to questions.

"How does Mrs. Jones know that she is going to get a baby?" "Why don't we get one?" "Why does a baby start to grow in one mother and not in another?" These and other similar questions are typical of the eight-year-old boy. Parents should be prepared to answer them simply and directly.

PARENT: Not all parents have babies the minute they want one. Sometimes they have to wait a long time before a baby grows.

BOY: Why?

PARENT: Each mother has one egg (or ovum) ripen each month. When it leaves the ovary, it must be joined with a sperm cell from the father or it won't grow into a baby.

BOY: Well then, why doesn't a baby grow if there is a mother and a father?

PARENT: A mother doesn't know the exact time an egg ripens. The little ovum is smaller than a grain of sand and can't be felt. A sperm is not always in a woman's body. Also, a wife and husband may want to wait until their own baby grows older before they plan to have another one.

BOY: Our baby is old enough to walk, and can even say some words. We could have another baby.

PARENT: Jimmy needs to be watched carefully, so he won't hurt himself. He still can't dress himself, go to the toilet, or bathe himself, eat alone, or take care of himself the way you do. I'm much too busy helping Jimmy grow up safely and happily, and seeing to it that you have everything you need, to have a helpless new infant right now.

BOY: I would help you. Honest I would!

PARENT: I'm sure you'd be a fine help, but you're at school and busy most of the day, and you have to have time to play outdoors with your friends. I don't think you could give me enough of your time to make both Jimmy and a new baby feel well cared for and content. And remember, our house has to be kept in order, and we all need to have clean clothes and good meals to eat.

BOY: Yeah, I suppose you're right. When Jimmy grows a little older, can we have another baby?

PARENT: That sounds like a good idea. We can talk more about it again when Jimmy gets a little older and can do more things for himself.

Children's questions

Some eight-year-old children are still searching for facts about babies, particularly relative to their starting, the length of a pregnancy, and how they are born. Boys generally want to know about the father's part in the growth of a baby, but usually are not as inquisitive as girls. When an adult can speak without embarrassment about the parts of the body and how they function—when words such as uterus, penis, ovary can be said as unemotionally as stomach, heart, and liver—the child in turn will feel comfortable asking any question he has concerning birth, babies, and sex. The adult's ease is contagious.

Some children would not dream of asking their parents anything relative to the subject, because they sense their parents' tension whenever the conversation even skirts the subject. Such parents often find it impossible to talk to their children about such ordinary functions as movement of the bowels and masturbation. They avoid their responsibilities by having their child discuss such things with their pediatrician, or cloak their own feelings behind crossness and scoldings when they are asked. These parents can overcome their own problems through reading and learning about the body systems. Reading the names of body parts and saying them aloud to themselves in the privacy of their own room helps them to get accustomed to the unfamiliar words. When the words can cross their lips easily, they are ready to try one out on their child.

To an eight-year-old, to hear, "The baby grows in the uterus, which is a special place were babies grow," is no more unusual than to say, "The esophagus is a tube through which food passes from the mouth to the stomach." As the parent gains an understanding of the amazing functioning of our body systems, he will also gain respect and appreciation for them. These attitudes of respect and appreciation are quickly caught by the children as they speak to their parents.

The rule of answering questions honestly and simply

continues at all age levels. The honest answers encourage a child to ask other questions he may have on the subject.

CHILD: Mother, how long does it take for a baby to grow?

MOTHER: About nine months for human beings.

CHILD: How do you know?

MOTHER: This has been thoroughly studied by doctors and scientists. They tell us that it usually takes nine months for the human baby to grow large enough to be born.

CHILD: It only took our chickens three weeks to grow in their eggs. Is that because we had them in an incubator?

MOTHER: They grew faster because chickens are very simple animals compared to people. Chickens live only a few years, while people live many years. We need a wonderful, complex body and a large, well-functioning brain to live the kind of life we do. How simple a chicken's life is compared to ours!

CHILD: A chicken hardly does anything, except eat, scratch, and lay eggs. They really are different from us! Do you know a chicken doesn't have to have his mother teach him to walk and eat? He can do it himself. My teacher said it's instinct that helps the chickens do those things.

The question of how a human baby is born and where it comes out of the body will be asked by some children who may have missed this learning earlier in life. The parent who hesitates in answering should be encouraged by knowing that the child is not shocked to learn about it. It is not enough to say, "It comes out through an opening between the mother's legs." The child may assume it comes out of the bowels via the anus, which would be shocking. It should be stressed that the baby has its very own birth canal.

PARENT: There is a very special birth canal called the vagina, which is between a mother's legs. This birth canal is used only for babies.

CHILD: *It must be an awful big birth canal, 'cause the baby isn't little-bitty like a mouse.*

PARENT: *Our bodies are very wonderfully made. That birth canal, which we call the vagina, is usually very small, but when a baby is being born it stretches large enough for the baby to be pushed through it. After the baby is born, it goes back to its usual size.*

CHILD: *What pushes the baby through the birth canal?*

PARENT: *Muscles. Muscles in the uterus start squeezing, and that pushes the baby into the vagina. The muscles push the baby slowly on out into the world.*

CHILD: *Andy said the doctor spanks the baby when it is born. Does he really do that?*

PARENT: *Well, it isn't a real "spanking." Doctors often give the baby a spank on the buttocks to start him breathing. While the baby was in the uterus he didn't breathe through his nose. He got everything he needed through the umbilical cord. When the baby is born he must breathe our air and get nourishment through his mouth. He no longer needs the umbilical cord.*

"How does a baby happen to grow in the uterus?" is another question which may be asked. It is necessary and good for children to know that Father plays a part in bringing this new life to the family.

CHILD: *When you get married does a baby start to grow?*

PARENT: *No, a baby only starts when a mother's ovum, or egg, unites with a sperm from the father.*

CHILD: *When does a daddy's sperm meet the egg?*

PARENT: *When a mother and father decide they want a baby, the father puts the sperm in mother.*

Girls seem to be more inquisitive than boys at this age. Bedtime often brings on a barrage of questions, for the goodnight ritual is a quiet, intimate time between parent and child. Girls are not only more inquisitive than the average boy of this age, but appear to accept the facts of reproduction more easily. The explanation that sperm cells leave the father's body through the penis and enter the mother's body when the father places his sex organ in the mother's, is usually accepted calmly by the daughter. If a boy should ask this question it may be answered in the same way.

Some parents, who are aware that their child is a human broadcasting station, need to teach him that discretion must be used as to what is told to people outside of the family. One such child told every detail of conversations he heard at home. The shocked parents began to get the echoes of their son's replays to interested friends. They had a family meeting, at which time they tried to help their child learn that some information, though important and interesting, was "family talk" and was not meant for outsiders' ears. The idea intrigued the young boy, and he often asked after that, "Can I tell Jimmy this, or is it family talk?" The parent who talks freely with his child about reproduction would be wise to label the discussion "family talk."

"It will be better if you don't tell your friends the things we're talking about," the mother may say. "You see, many parents want to tell their children themselves, and they know when their child is mature enough to understand. Our little Jimmy isn't old enough for this kind of discussion, so let's wait until he gets to be as old as you are."

Many a mother is asked loudly in a public lavatory, "What's in here? Can I have one?" Such a place does not lend itself to explanations about sanitary napkins. Mother may tell her child that she will be happy to tell her at home. This promise must be kept. Explaining to her daughter later that the pad is something women need during the menstruation period because there is a little discharge from the uterus, and that this discharge is absorbed by the sanitary pad, usually will satisfy the child's curiosity.

At school

The eight-year-old child enjoys school, because he likes being with children his own age. He is not as dependent on the teacher as he was at an earlier age. She is less important to his well-being, and he can accept a more impersonal approach with her. He enjoys adult-type conversations with his teacher and still seeks her praise for work that is well done. When his efforts in arithmetic or on a test do not measure up to his standards, or he needs to be disciplined, he often will complain of headaches or stomachaches. These are safe symptoms to have, for what teacher or parent can prove that Johnny does not have a headache or stomachache?

Teachers find the eight-year-old a social person, eager to be involved in school activities, liking small-group endeavors, anxious to join the spelling club or be chairman of the classroom library committee.

Learning about family patterns

Eight- and nine-year-old children often become involved in learning about early man and about people in other lands in their classroom studies. Social studies often overlap with units in science and in family living, as well as history and geography.

As children read and learn about early man, they enjoy comparing the primitive life of the cave man with our present-day family life. Their questions are many. Did the cave man have a family unit with a mother, a father, and children? Why did they dress in animal skins? What was the role of the father? Was he well suited for his tasks? What did the mother do? How did these early people get married? There were no hospitals, so how did the mothers have their babies? If the fathers did not earn money, how did they provide for their families?

Trying to find the answers to these questions can prove to be a challenge and stimulant to the inquisitive mind of the small child.

Play-acting or writing stories about what it would have been like to be a girl or boy in a cave family helps children gain an understanding of early man's needs and desires. In comparing the clothing of early man and woman, they discover that the clothing of the two sexes was similar. Why do boys and girls and men and women of today dress differently than each other? Does our climate dictate how we dress?

As the children learn about cultures of other lands, they are surprised to discover that not all family patterns are just like ours. The Masai in Kenya, Africa, find it acceptable and practical for a man to have more than one family, for their needs are different from ours. The early Mormons in our country found it moral and right for a man to have several wives. Some children may point out that the Old Testament often tells of a man having several wives. Critical analysis and decisions are made by young children as they ponder these facts.

Learning to understand the reasons for the differences in clothing in the many climatic regions of the world, determining why many Japanese people of today dress in Western clothes while others continue wearing the traditional Japanese type of clothing, is fascinating. At this age, imaginations are unlimited and powers of reasoning are growing, providing ever-improving abilities to work out solutions to questions and problems.

Children also discover not only that there are different kinds of families right in our own neighborhoods, but that the differences become even greater from country to country. They soon reach the conclusion that man must do what is best for his culture and climate.

However, most children are greatly relieved that they live in our country and in our time.

Science

Science continues to provide many opportunities to study animal reproduction as children learn about mammals, insects, and birds. They reinforce earlier learning that all animal life must reproduce if it is to continue to exist. Children rediscover that all animal life starts as an egg, and the egg must be fertilized with a sperm to develop new life. They learn that a mammal's egg is fertilized internally, because the new life develops and grows inside of the mother and is born alive. (Many children are quick to point out that the platypus is a mammal that lays eggs.)

Children may ask the teacher how the sperm cell gets into the female's body to fertilize the egg.

TEACHER: *The male animal has a special opening in his body, which he puts next to a special opening in the female's body. At this time the tiny sperm cells, which are in a liquid called semen, pass from the male animal's body into the female's body.*
CHILD: *Where is the opening?*
TEACHER: *Between the hind legs of most animals. When animals do this we say they are mating. Do you think that animals know that they are starting new life when they mate?*
CHILD: *No, they do things by instinct.*
TEACHER: *Right, their instinct has them do the necessary things to live and to reproduce new life.*

Most children are curious about how long it takes for a baby to develop inside of the mother before it is ready to be born. Some children can make a graph to show the period of gestation for various mammals. This information may be found in books. The cat is usually born sixty days after conception, the dog in sixty-three days, while the horse takes three hundred and thirty-five days and the elephant six hundred and sixty-five. Some children will enjoy finding information on how different animals care for their young, and how long the babies depend on their parents or parent for care.

Learning the correct names of the reproductive organs of animals, and comparing ways in which animals reproduce, helps children gain a frame of reference for discussing physiology and anatomy. *Ovary, ova, ovum, uterus, sperm, semen, umbilical cord, navel, birth canal, vagina, embryo, breasts*—all are words children quickly learn and use.

The film, *Animal Reproduction*, by Coronet Films, shows animals being born. This film is best shown after the children have had the basic understanding developed through discussion and reading. The teacher should make sure all the children viewing the film understand that the baby mammal is being born through the vagina and not out through the rectum and the anus.

Animals reproduce their own kind. This fact needs to be pointed out by the teacher: a dog never gives birth to kittens, an elephant never has a giraffe, a bee never has a wasp, but each animal continues his own kind on earth.

Human beings reproduce

The strong interest in how a mother has a baby subsides somewhat at this age. However, a teacher must be ready to answer questions asked by children who are awakening to the interest in human reproduction later than the average child. The teacher also may find that some children will be aware of the similarity between human reproduction and that of other mammals.

ELIZABETH: *I started from a tiny egg and sperm just like the whale and the baby calf did.*

TEACHER: *That's right. All mammals start that way. Do you know why we start life in the same way as other mammals?*

BILL: *I do! It's because we're mammals, too.*

TEACHER: *Yes, we are mammals.*

BILL: *But we're smarter than all the other mammals.*

TEACHER: *Do you know why we are smarter?*

BILL: *We have a bigger and better brain.*

TEACHER: *That's right, Bill. Because we have a better brain, is our life different from that of other mammals?*

ELIZABETH: *It's very different. We can plan and think about what we do. Mammals do things by instinct.*

TEACHER: *Is it instinct that makes a mother dog care for her puppies?*

JANE: *It's instinct. She never was taught how to carry her babies and feed her babies; she just does it.*

TEACHER: *Why does your mother feed and take care of you and your family? Is that instinct?*

JANE: *She loves us, and she learned how to do it.*

TEACHER: *Other mammals are like us in many ways, but very, very different in some ways. People can feel love and responsibility for each other.*

This type of conversation will arise often, if children are given the opportunity to talk freely in the classroom and ask questions. Also, the teacher's questions can stimulate children to explore the subject further.

In learning about the method of reproduction of animals, the question may be asked concerning fertilization of the egg in human beings.

ALAN: *How does the sperm fertilize the egg in the mother?*

TEACHER: *Do you remember how the fish eggs were fertilized by the sperm?*

ALAN: *Yes, the female laid the eggs in the water, and the male laid his sperm over the eggs.*

TEACHER: *That's right. Do you remember how the cow's egg was fertilized?*

ALAN: *Inside her body, because the baby grows in her uterus.*

TEACHER: How did the sperm get to the egg?

ALAN: The male put his sperm cells in the mother's body.

TEACHER: You remember so well, Alan. Now, do you remember what we called it when the male put the sperm cells in the female's vagina?

ALAN: Yeah, they were mating. Hey, is that how the sperm cells get in the mother's body to fertilize the egg?

TEACHER: A mother and father must mate, too, to start new life. But their mating is very different in a very special way. Animals mate because of—

ALAN: Instinct!

TEACHER: That's right, because of instinct. People mate because they love each other. When a wife and husband love each other very much, they often want children of their very own to love and care for. They want a new life that is their very own to love and to cherish. In your family that very special life is you.

ALAN: Yeah! And my baby brother, too.

Many eight- and nine-year-old children, particularly girls, know how human babies are born. Other eight-year-olds are not interested in all the details of how the muscles of the uterus push the baby out, or of how the placenta is pushed out. Their main concern is where the babies come out.

JIMMY: How do people's babies get out of the mother's uterus?

JANE: Everyone knows that! They come out a special birth canal.

TEACHER: Yes Jane, human babies come out a special birth canal called the vagina. The opening is between the mother's legs. The birth canal is not used for anything except babies. Does that answer your question, Jimmy?

JIMMY: Yes, but doesn't the baby have to be awful skinny to come out that way?

TEACHER: No, it doesn't, Jimmy. The vagina stretches like a rubber balloon, big enough for the baby to get through. After the baby is born, the vagina goes back to its small size.

There are two kinds of animals on earth. Who can tell me the two kinds?

PATTY: Male and female.

TEACHER: There are two kinds of every mammal on earth.

JANE: I know! Male and female.

TEACHER: There are two kinds of Eskimos.

JOHN: Male and female.

TEACHER: There are two kinds of Chinese.

ALAN: Male and female.

TEACHER: And two kinds of people in this room.

ALL THE CHILDREN: We know! Male and female.

TEACHER: Yes, all the people in the world are either male or female. We all look different on the outside, for our hair and eyes and skins are different shades of color. My nose is a different shape from Jane's, Mary is taller than Ann, but inside we are all pretty much the same. Some of us are females and the rest are males.

Chapter Nine

The Nine-Year-Old
at Home

Behavior at nine

Self-motivation is a noticeable characteristic of the nine-year-old child. The school skill subjects of reading, mathematics, and writing are often attacked with a greater degree of interest than formerly, and with longer periods of concentration. Nine is more realistic than the seven- and eight-year-old child and is learning self-criticism. He usually is first to admit that he is having trouble with a particular school subject, and is willing to drill himself because of his desire to improve.

Nine likes to classify and identify cars, ball teams, jets, birds, stamps, and any other special interests he may have. Often he appears to be a genius in the eyes of doting parents, as he expounds the batting averages of innumerable baseball stars or explains in detail the color and uniqueness of each state's automobile license plate.

Infantile alibi-ing is slowly slipping away, and the ability to accept blame is gradually being learned at nine years of age; but "being fair" is becoming an obsession and nine insists all blame be fairly distributed in a group misdemeanor, with emphasis laid upon the person or event that started the difficulty.

Girls are beginning to appear and act more adult than boys, for girls are nearer the age of puberty than boys. They are interested in caring for their own hair and often have firm opinions on how it should be styled. The type of clothes they wear is beginning to take on more importance.

Most boys continue to be generally careless about appearance and seldom arrive home from school with shirts neatly tucked under their belts. Some boys, however, discover that carefully combed hair makes them appear older and more attractive. They insist on carrying a pocket comb, and seem to be constantly wetting their hair and plastering it down. This stage of neatness rarely lasts long.

Nine is anxious to prove to himself and others that he is maturing. He makes many fewer demands on his parents, and in turn wants fewer demands made on him. Yet nine is careless and forgets to brush his teeth, hang up his clothes, put his schoolbooks away, or wash his hands before eating. Since constant requests annoy him, he often reacts more positively to a written list of duties. Checking the chart each time he brushes his teeth or cleans up his room is more acceptable than verbal reminders. Many parents have found that a system of fining brings better results than nagging a child of this age. Taking away a privilege, such as watching TV, until his room is cleaned is also effective.

The child and family

The nine-year-old does not demand as much attention or time of his mother as previously. He is busy and self-centered and more able to entertain himself in the home. He may read for hours, or spend an entire morning with his electric train. The girls still enjoy dolls, particularly the small dolls with large wardrobes or paper dolls with many types of clothing. Some girls become budding dress designers while playing with paper dolls.

The mother who treats her nine-year-old with respect according to his increased maturity will find a smooth relationship; the mother who demands neatness, immediate obedience to directions, and points out the child's every fault, may soon have a bold, saucy, and irritable child. Asking a child to carry out the garbage in the same manner and tone of voice as with an adult usually results in a receptive child. If he is permitted to choose the time convenient to him, he will be even more willing.

The father, too, will have smooth sailing if he respects his child's increased maturity. A boy often seeks a closer relationship with his father at this age, and wants his father to have a good opinion of him and is very sensitive to any criticism from him. He admires his father's ability to understand technical subjects and wants to know about his work. He often puts his father on a pedestal and boasts shamelessly to his friends about how great his father is and the success he has!

Special family projects can be enjoyed by both the nine-year-old and his parents, if the adults adhere to a respectful but firm manner with their child. When on a vacation trip, many children want to haunt all the souvenir shops. One girl's parents solved the problem of their child's wanting dozens of knicknacks (which the parents felt were a waste of money), by giving their daughter three dollars to spend in any way she wished. It was made clear to her that the money must last for the entire trip. The journeys through the shops continued, but she never found a trinket on which she was willing to spend her precious souvenir fund. The unpleasant "begging" ceased, and the child, happily clutching her purse with the three dollars, enjoyed the shops as much as she had previously.

Another set of parents were told how well the plan

had worked and decided to try the system with their nine-year-old son. The boy immediately insisted that three dollars bought nothing valuable and the least his parents could do was raise the sum to five dollars. The boy understood his parents well. He knew they were never firm about decisions and rules concerning him; therefore he quickly spent his five dollars on trifles and continued to beg for more. As he also foresaw, the parents did not stick to their ultimatum; they listened to his pleas and bought him all he wanted.

Upon their return home, the parents enjoyed telling how clever their son was and how softhearted they were. They were convinced that such a plan as they had tried did not work—for had they not proved it unsuccessful?

Some nines enjoy parent or family excursions, but if faced with a decision to go to the beach with the family or play with a group of best friends, often choose their peers. Parents occasionally find their child's decision annoying; they discover it difficult to accept that their precious offspring has preferred the company of friends to that of parents. Instead of jealousy, parents should feel pride that they have raised a normal child who is slowly weaning himself away from the need for constant parental attention.

Peer groups

Nine gets along well with his peers. Play is accompanied by incessant talk, which can hardly be referred to as conversation for it sounds more like choral speaking. In spite of the fact that the children seem to be all speaking at once, they apparently are communicating with one another.

Short-lived clubs continue to be formed. They rarely get beyond the planning stages of deciding upon secret meeting places, secret passwords, and the coining of new words to be used for sending coded messages. Adult-led

Cub Scouts and Girl Scouts appeal to many children.

Most boys and girls enjoy group games together, when under the direction of an adult leader. Although there is usually a friendly attitude between the boys and girls, they seldom choose voluntarily to play together. A few nine-year-olds dislike the opposite sex. "I hate boys" or "I hate girls" is often verbalized by these children.

Boys of nine enjoy games that involve roughhousing, wrestling, and much running. Girls, too, have an abundance of energy, but more often choose quiet games. A dress-up box may be the start of a neighborhood dramatic performance such as a circus, carnival, or play. More time is spent in planning how much the admittance price will be, making tickets, making posters, and deciding who will perform and what they will do, than on the final performance.

Outlets for tension

The excessive activity of the nine-year-old child helps him to rid himself of many tensions through his physical exertion. Boys, in particular, often annoy adults, for they seem to be constantly on the move and are forever pulling, pushing, or tripping other children. When they are expected to sit quietly at home or at school, they seem to find release by shuffling their feet, cracking their knuckles, biting their nails, or playing with their hair.

Nine usually is a good sleeper, but may have scary dreams occasionally. When awakened by a parent, he realizes that he has been dreaming and quiets down quickly. He also understands that a scary TV show or movie may be the cause of his nightmare.

Jean discovered that she always had bad dreams after seeing something frightening in a dramatic performance. She was so thoroughly convinced that this was the cause that, when a program on TV had a part she found objectionable, she would run out of the room. At the theater she would tell her friends she was going to the washroom or to get a drink, and would stay there until she felt the scary part was over. At nine, she was able to recognize her problem and find a solution that she felt helped her.

Some nine-year-old children are anxious and apprehensive about themselves. They may worry about their health and wonder why their legs get pains in them, why they get a headache, why their stomach hurts. These children are often helped if they realize that they are not the only child with these symptoms. A perceptive doctor may be able to help the child to understand better the causes of these pains and help him to realize that they are not necessarily serious. The parent should not show alarm or be overly solicitous about these vague aches, for this apprehension can lead the child to becoming a chronic complainer and worrier. If a physical examination reveals no serious problems, parents should treat complaints lightly. They may say, "I'm sorry you have a headache. Why not lie down on the sofa a few minutes? A short rest should help." This assures the child that his parent is sympathetic but not alarmed by his condition.

Parents, however, must be alert to a child's persistent lament. John's mother was sure her child had become a hypochondriac, for he complained of frequent stomachaches. The attack seemed to become worse when it was time for school or time to undertake some task he disliked. John was taken to the doctor by his annoyed mother, for she was sure he used the ailment as an escape device to avoid what he found frustrating. The doctor was not convinced that the problem was imaginary and ordered tests made at the hospital. John had an ulcer!

"I'm the dumbest kid in class," or "Boy, I'm really stupid!" should not be ignored when a child sincerely feels this indicates his overall performance at school.

The poor opinion he has of his ability may be a cry for help. The parent should confer with the teacher and try to explore the reasons for this poor self-evaluation. The child may need to progress more slowly at school and be given an opportunity to catch up. Counseling by the school social worker may help him to gain a better self-image, or tutoring may strengthen his learning. When a child consistently feels he is failing, steps must be taken immediately to help him.

Most children will occasionally say, "Boy, am I dumb!" in a joking manner, when they discover that they have made a careless mistake. This form of self-teasing is not to be confused with a child's earnest appraisal of generally poor attainment.

Nine and sex

Nine becomes more interested in his own sex and function of sex organs than in the opposite sex. Girls often question whether they will have babies when they grow up, and when they need to wear a bra. Some become very modest and do not want their father or even baby brother to see them dressing. They may request that even Mother should knock before entering, for they prefer to have clothes on when she comes into the room. It is not unusual for girls to insist upon wearing panties under their pajama pants. This phase of excessive modesty is usually temporary, but indicates that the child is maturing mentally and becoming more aware of her body.

Boys, too, are more modest at this age and often have spells of not wanting any female—mother or baby sister —around when nude. Mothers who insist on entering upon the bath to supervise should give thought to changing feelings that come to children at various stages of growth. A bit of unscrubbed skin is better than upsetting a sudden spell of modesty. In contrast, some nine-year-old boys are completely oblivious of their bodies and would not flinch if the neighbor lady came into the room during bath time. These changing moods of a growing child are not predictable or constant in all children.

The division of sexes in play is normal at this time, yet there is usually an awareness of the opposite sex. This is often demonstrated by the teasing that takes place. "Mary loves Alan," "I hate Mary," "I love you," "Tim kissed Jean," are typical of notes written and passed between children or boldly scribbled on sidewalks.

A boy and girl who find themselves together and apart from others, often can play and talk harmoniously together. Lisa and Andy had to stay in the classroom and miss gym class one day, due to temporary physical ailments restricting their running. They asked the teacher if they could hold one of the seven-day-old baby chicks. Before long the two children were happily sitting on the floor enjoying the chick's antics. They were so involved in the joy of feeling and watching the newly hatched chickens that they were unaware of the usual disdain they had for each other. The minute the class returned from gym, Lisa and Andy again joined their own sex.

Many parents who have tried to have a party with both sexes have found it soon became a complete disaster. The boys would decide to kiss the girls (or the girls would decide to kiss the boys) for an added bit of fun, and the chase began. Normally well-behaved children ran wildly through the rooms, screaming as though being murdered.

Need for guidance

Nine-year-old children who have received information about the growth and birth of babies at an earlier age show less interest in reproduction. If they find a book of anatomy with pictures showing the various parts of the body, preferably their own sex, they study the pictures with interest. Parents may expect more questions concerning their child's own sex than about reproduction. The mother is most often asked questions by both sexes, since she is with the children more often than the father.

CHILD: *Will my penis grow like Dad's?*

ADULT: *Yes, it will grow larger as you mature.*

CHILD: *How old will I be then?*

ADULT: *Well, all boys don't mature at exactly the same age. Some mature when they are twelve and some when they are as old as sixteen or seventeen.*

CHILD: *That's funny. Why don't we all mature at the same time?*

ADULT: *Growth patterns vary. Some children grow tall when they are thirteen, fourteen, or fifteen, and then stop. Some children stay small until they are sixteen or eighteen, and then they start to grow very fast. Sometimes the late growers get taller than the boys who did their growing at fourteen and fifteen. That's just the way growth patterns are.*

CHILD: *How old do you think I'll be when I start to grow tall?*

ADULT: *That's hard to predict. If you follow your father's growth pattern, you'll do most of your maturing and growing when you're around sixteen or seventeen. In fact, your father was still getting taller when he went to college, and he grew bigger shoulders, too.*

Some boys experiment with swearwords at this age. These words are often connected with sex or elimination and are usually learned from their peers. The children are certain that they will impress others with how grown up, rough, and tough they are by using these newly learned "bad words."

If ignored, the words may soon be forgotten. Some children will persist, however, especially if their peers have been impressed by them. Parents certainly have the right and duty to stop their use in the home.

FATHER: Tom, swearwords are not allowed in our home. Neither Mother nor I use them, because we find them offensive. You are not to use them either.

SON: Heck! All the boys say those words.

FATHER: The other boys are not our son and do not live in our home.

SON: Well, I don't know why you have to be different from other parents. They don't stop their kids.

FATHER: Other parents have a right to make their own rules about such matters. Mother and I have a right to make our rules. In our house there will be no swearing.

SON: Can I swear when I'm not at home?

FATHER: If you want people to know you are a child who swears, then go right ahead. Mother and I don't like swearwords.

SON: Huh, I bet you'll get mad if I swear when I'm away from home!

FATHER: It certainly would not make Mother or me happy to know that you choose to swear. But you must make your own decision about what you do, for Mother and I aren't planning to follow you around all day. As you get older and more independent, you'll have to make more and more decisions for yourself. Mother and I want to help you learn to make good decisions, for this will help you grow into a strong and intelligent adult.

The ages between seven and ten are most important to a child for growth in the ability to make good decisions independently, and in gaining self-discipline. When a child develops these important character qualities, there is little chance of his becoming a delinquent in his teen years.

A child this age needs continuous guidance by parents, yet they must be alert to the maturing that is taking place. Guidance is not the same as insisting upon good behavior in children through constant vigilance and strictness. An oversolicitous parent may teach Mary to be a puppet, unable to make decisions for herself and relying upon a parent to pave the way for her. Mary often finds schoolwork too taxing and depends upon the step-by-step help of the parent to write papers, do arithmetic assignments, and learn the words on the spelling lists. She may be unable to cope with the world when the time comes for her to leave the nest.

An overstrict, demanding parent subjects the child to his will. Again, the child is not learning to reach for good behavior on his own. He is intimidated by the iron rule of someone stronger than he. He too may become an obedient puppet; or he may become angry and rebellious, and take out his frustrations on people outside of the home.

In contrast to the overzealous parent is the mother who thoroughly enjoys her new freedom away from the constant supervision she needed to give her little children. She may forget that her preteen child still needs continuous adult guidance.

Chris's mother does not know where he is when away from home. He is permitted to be so independent that he is able to get into trouble without his mother being aware of it, unless a neighbor calls to inform her. Chris often feels neglected and unloved, through his abandonment by his mother, and is becoming an angry, belligerent child. He often boasts about the fact that he can do anything he wants to; but he really does not feel he is fortunate to have such unlimited freedom, nor is it bringing him security and happiness.

Carol is being weaned away slowly from the constant supervision she needed when younger. She is permitted to make many small decisions for herself. Her ability to judge wisely is noted by her parents, and she is aware of their approval. As she grows in her ability to make good decisions, her parents allow her an increasing degree of independence.

Carol proved to her mother that she could take the

bus alone to the stores, which are a ten-minute ride from home. When she shopped for clothes with her mother, she was encouraged to seek out the dresses, underwear, and socks she liked. Then she and her mother would discuss the price, quality, and style, and together make the decision whether to buy it or not.

When Carol was nine, she asked for permisson ito have her own charge plate and be permitted to purchase some items alone. The store agreed that Carol seemed responsible enough to care for a charge plate. It was a monumental day when for the first time she took the bus and bought some socks with her own charge plate. On returning home she proudly displayed her purchase and put the charge plate safely in the predetermined place in her mother's desk.

At a later date, Carol's mother visited the store and spoke to the saleswoman about her daughter's first independent shopping experience. As she expected, the saleswoman gave a glowing report of Carol's responsible behavior and courtesy. Carol took pride in her parents' confidence, which she earned by demonstrating her ability to use her growing maturity wisely. Slowly, her independence grew along with her desire to make wise and good decisions.

When the time arrives for Carol to leave home to go to college or find a job, she will continue to feel her parents' guidance and trust, and these will influence her adjustment to her new environment.

Boys should be boys

Some parents are extremely anxious to teach their boy to be a real boy, to a degree which may deny him some interesting experiences. Learning to make fudge or pancakes is often enjoyed by boys and men, and does not label a boy "sissy."

Parents should be concerned, however, if a nine- or ten-year-old boy continues "playing house" with girls in preference to joining a group of boys at play. Parents should also be alert to a girl or boy who has not been able to make friends with children of his own age and sex, and seeks refuge at home to avoid admitting the lack of friends. The need for help is indicated for these children.

Summer camp, preferably away from home, classes at a boys' club or a girls' club, offer opportunities to learn to play with others. If this does not help, the school social worker or other professional person's advice should be sought.

It is often difficult for parents to look at their son or daughter objectively. Love, pride, and enjoyment of one's own child may blind parents to his needs. Jimmy was such a child. He was a chubby, smiling boy, nearing the age of ten. Adults found him delightful, for he was thoughtful and polite and thoroughly enjoyed conversing with them. He was an above-average student at school, with exemplary behavior in the classroom.

Jimmy's parents found him a joy around the house. The father was gone all week as a salesman, spending only Saturday and Sunday at home; Jimmy was a true blessing to his mother, for he willingly helped her with countless household chores. He delighted in baking cookies and cakes, which gave him the opportunity of nibbling and adding countless calories to his already more than adequate daily intake of food.

Jimmy's mother was particularly grateful to have such a companionable son, for she was experiencing a rather difficult pregnancy and he was a great comfort and aid to her. Her one fear was that, due to her close relationship with Jimmy, he would resent any encroachment on her time by the new baby. Her fears were unfounded. Jimmy added care of the baby to his home activities.

He took his baby sister for daily walks in her carriage, and was proud of all the admiring comments made by the neighbor women.

The classroom teacher began to be disturbed by Jimmy's lack of companionship at school. He appeared to be content, but was seldom seen talking to other boys. When committees were formed or teams chosen in gym classes, Jimmy was always the last to be selected. The teacher noticed that he arrived at school and left by himself, while others raced happily about in clusters. At the next parent-teacher conference, Jimmy's mother was asked about his after-school activities and his friends. As the mother began to tell about his friends and activities, it was becoming evident that his friends were adults and his baby sister.

"Jimmy tells me so much about Gary and Stan. Doesn't he play with them?" asked the mother.

"Not at school. He's alone during the periods of the day when children normally visit together. Does he play with them or other boys after school?" asked the teacher.

"Well, no. He's usually around the house after school, busy with something every minute. We thought he had plenty of friendships and play during school. I'm beginning to think that I've been unaware of my son's lack of friends. Goodness, what should I do?" added the mother with sudden panic.

At the teacher's suggestion, the school social worker and the family pediatrician were consulted by the parents. Classmates were invited over after school. The father took Jimmy and a friend to a baseball game, and he found more time to spend with his son on weekends. The baby sister still enjoyed her brother during the shorter periods of time she spent with him. A boys' camp was carefully chosen and Jimmy gradually gained techniques in playing boys' games and in making friends with his peers. Fortunately for Jimmy, concerned adults helped him and guided him into a more boy-oriented environment.

Girls should be girls

Jane was born to parents who had waited long for a child; in fact they had given up hopes of ever having one. When the new father had been told that his long-awaited son and heir was a girl, he was deeply disappointed. Coming from a family of six boys, he had been so sure that he, too, would have a son. His first wave of disappointment soon passed, as he became acquainted with his beautiful baby daughter.

Jane's uncle and aunt lived next door with their five boys, whose ages ranged from six months to twelve years. The boys adored their new cousin and begged to hold her. Jane's mother soon began to dress her baby daughter in the "hardly worn" leftover clothes from the boy cousins. The economy was not necessary, but it seemed ridiculous to refuse the offer of clothes. "After all," she told her husband, "they're attractive, and Jane certainly doesn't miss ribbons and ruffles." As Jane grew older she continued to wear boys' coats, jackets, hats, and sweaters. She even wore boys' slacks for play.

The boy cousins particularly enjoyed Jane when she reached the toddling stage. They never seemed to tire of giving her piggyback rides, and soon Jane joined them in their roughhousing. As she grew older, she spent most of her playtime with her cousins. Jane's father was proud of her ability to hold her own with all the boys. His games with his young daughter were all the rough-and-tumble kinds he knew from his own childhood in his boy-centered home.

Doting grandparents had given Jane dolls and a beautiful dollhouse, but after the first thrill of ownership Jane neglected her girl-toys. No one thought of playing with her and helping her learn how to enjoy her new dollhouse. She naturally preferred playing with people, and so continued to choose the boy-type games her cousins liked; and she would play any game to please her father and get his attention.

Jane's father soon boasted that, "Jane hasn't time for girl things, like dolls. She prefers balls and bats. She's a real tomboy!"

When Jane entered school the boys were her main friends. She was a happy, well-liked member of her class, but noticeably boyish in her mannerisms and interests. She hated dresses, which she had to wear to school. No effort seemed to be made to choose dresses of attractive styles or colors, and no feminine accessories were added.

The third-grade teacher, who recognized Jane's need to be more involved with her own sex, suggested to the parents that some feminine activities be provided for her. They immediately enrolled her in a ballet class, and she joined a Brownie troop. She mildly enjoyed the dancing class, but the ballet dress looked strange on her. Her boyish gait and movements did not suit the picture of a ballerina. Brownies soon bored Jane, and she quit. The activities were all geared to girl interests. The members of the troop liked Jane's easygoing, friendly manner, but they seldom invited her to their homes more than once or twice.

In high school Jane did not lack for friends, but neither did she have a best friend like most of the girls and boys. The boys all liked her, but never chose her for their date. Her parents were not alarmed when she announced that she thought high-school dating stupid. They were secretly relieved that they did not have the usual concerns most parents have with their daughters, and were confident that she would find dating interesting when she was older.

After five months at college, she came zooming home on her motorcycle and announced that she was through with school. She didn't like the college kids. "All the girls could think about was boys and getting pinned or married, and the boys were just as bad! The classes were stupid and a waste of time," she insisted. So Jane was home to stay, disappointed with people and college.

The parents finally became concerned and wondered what had gone wrong at college that caused their "well-adjusted" child to be completely disillusioned. Not once did it occur to them that they had played any part in Jane's failure in college life.

Listen, learn, and guide

Some parents guide their children's interests and activities by listening to them with enthusiasm and respect. Through listening, they discover the appropriate time to encourage their child, to make suggestions that help boost him over a difficult barrier, and to recognize improvement or a job well done.

Peter had an amazing fund of knowledge about animals because of his intense curiosity and his parents' support and guidance. He lived in a big city where most adults feel that wildlife is nonexistent, except for the city zoo. Peter's home, which he shared with a brother, two sisters, and his parents, was in a typical big-city neighborhood of houses and apartments. There was still one vacant, uncared-for lot near his home, which the adults resented and the children loved. The children had beaten a pathway diagonally through it on the theory that it was a shortcut to wherever they were going.

The children all ran wild through the small parcel of land that to them spelled freedom, Indians, and pioneers. Peter, too, found that special piece of ground adventurous, but his eyes did not see Indians. It was the earth's little creatures that held him spellbound: the beetle that stayed at the edge of the path to avoid running feet, the worm that floated to the surface during a pelting rain, the ants carrying their life-giving burdens, the garden snake that found the protection of the tall weeds his refuge, the cricket that sang his joyous song under a piece of discarded candy wrapper.

One cricket found its way into Peter's hand, which eagerly held the insect captive until a suitable home was found. The little wax begonia which bloomed cheerily in the kitchen window was just the right home for the little cricket, Peter's mother decided. She found that the chimney from her hurricane lamp fit perfectly over begonia and cricket. She then cut a small circle of mesh from an old stocking of hers, which she placed on top of the chimney. She secured it in place with a rubberband, and imprisoned the little animal.

The cricket found his new home delightful and enjoyed his bits of wool yarn, raw apple, and other small tidbits of food Peter dropped into the cage. He scraped his wings in thankful appreciation to Peter and his mother. The family enjoyed the cricket and his cheerful chirping song. Peter and his father searched for books about crickets on their next weekly visit to the public library. Together they learned how crickets live, eat, reproduce, and make the familiar cricket sounds of late summer.

Peter, of course, added more crickets to keep his new pet from getting lonesome. Soon he learned, in horror, that two males could not live peacefully in his small cage, for they fought until one was killed and partially devoured by the victor. The females munched contentedly on the fruit and begonia leaves, unaware of the males' battle for the harem. The victorious male lived his short life happily with the egg-laying females.

It was Peter who suggested that the books should tell the whole story of crickets. Not one book had mentioned that the males would fight and try to kill the contender who wanted the females to be his mates.

Peter was witness to the fact that the females force

the long, needlelike egg layers at the rear of their bodies into the soft soil. One obligingly laid her eggs right next to the glass of the chimney, and Peter saw the many minute eggs. As fall arrived, sending many animals to their winter homes, the crickets died (as all crickets do) despite their summerlike environment. As a living testimony to their existence the bedraggled, well-chewed begonia held on to life tenaciously and slowly grew strong and beautiful once again.

One spring morning, as the family was enjoying breakfast, Peter was the one who noticed the cricket cage filled with tiny hopping specks. The eggs had hatched!

Peter had cages about his home all during his childhood. His tolerant parents must have found the many insects and animals with which they shared their home annoying at times, but they placed their child's interests and desires above their own. There were ant villages in big two-quart pickle jars, a snake in an old aquarium which had been converted into a woodland terrarium, frogs and toads living in a child-created cage, and fruit-fly and meal-worm cultures, producing food for the small worm- and insect-eating animals.

Peter watched the habits of his many pets. His parents guided him in finding books at the library telling about the animals he had. He learned how the animals existed, what they ate, how they reproduced, what enemies they had, what value they had for man—or how they harmed man.

The family made a point of becoming acquainted with the forest preserve near their home, visiting the zoo and learning about the animals, and driving out to the country to explore farms. Summer vacations often were spent camping in the woods next to a small lake, and investigating every part of the surroundings.

Peter's father helped him to see the many birds that were in the trees about his city home. Contrary to the common belief that only sparrows and starlings can exist in the city, Peter and his father discovered dozens of different kinds of birds that were high in the trees. They found the nighthawks in their daytime sleeping hideaways, and even an old whippoorwill sleeping contentedly, knowing that he blended with the bough on which he was flattened. During migration time the skies were watched for the millions of birds following their annual flyways. Peter and his father gathered books and articles which told of the thousands of miles many birds travel each spring and fall, where they spend their winters and summers, why birds migrate, and how they find their way.

There came a time when Peter began teaching his parents about animals. He told them how to track animals, which trees house opossums or raccoons (their homes can be discovered by a hair or two caught in the bark), and where and when to find frog, toad, and salamander eggs. Word spread about young Peter's interest, patience, and knowledge about animals. He fell heir to many animals people found: a barn owl with a broken wing caused by some hunter's carelessness and greedy shooting habits, a talking crow that must have escaped from his owner, a baby bird that seemed unattended, a baby squirrel found shivering on a parkway. Peter raised many animals on doll-baby bottles, with formulas similar to his baby sister's. Most of these animals were released in the forest preserve when old enough to find their own food, but one albino opossum was tamed and became a household pet.

Peter read in a scientific magazine about albino animals, and though he was only twelve years old at the time, he wrote to the author of the article telling him about his albino opossum. The author answered his letter, and between them they schemed to try to find a male albino opossum. Peter actually managed to find this rarity and hoped he would grow and mate with his female opossum. The male, however, died before he had a chance to discover whether the female albino was attractive, and the big experiment failed.

Later, Peter gave his beautiful white opossum, with a huge red ribbon tied into a bow around her neck, to the city traveling zoo. Hundreds of children were able to pet and enjoy Peter's unusual pet.

Chapter Ten

The Nine-Year-Old
at School

Behavior at school

Nine-year-old children usually enjoy school because they
like being with other children. They are quick to tell
the teacher that she is nice, if they like her, and enjoy
staying after school to help and talk to her. Many approach their school work with enthusiasm and are eager
to make improvement in skill subjects.

The desire of many nines to make lists of various
items, to classify, and to zero in on one specific interest,
can be a great aid to the teacher if she will plan to use
this special interest in her approach to learning. Intro-
ducing these children to a subject such as astronomy
can be an awe-inspiring experience to a new teacher
who has had no previous introduction to nine's interest
in lists and categories. Within days, many of the children list and learn the names of planets, their relationship to the sun, their distance from it, their size, the
number of moons of a particular planet, its estimated
temperature, and other endless information.

Astronomical numbers may amaze the teacher, but
her pupils use them without hesitation. To them a

trillion means "an awful lot," while the teacher admits to not being able to comprehend such a figure.

Nine-year-olds like to do research on a special subject, use an encyclopedia or book for information, and then report to the class. They are shameless plagiarists, and it takes great effort and patience on the part of the teacher to help them learn to put information gained from their reading into their own words. Their convincing argument for copying is, "But the book says it just the way I would say it!"

Learning about the family

Study of the family and reproduction can again be a part of the social studies, science, and health curriculums. The family can be studied as it relates to social studies. If early America happens to be the unit under consideration, children may read, learn, discuss, and compare the needs and desires of the early settler's family with the family of today. In comparing the pioneer family with today's family, the children will discover that many of the needs are the same and many totally different.

The needs that remain the same are the role of the father and mother in bringing new life into the world, the family's need for love and security, and the need for food and clothing and shelter.

Many needs of the self-sufficient extended pioneer family, as compared with today's smaller dependent family, are different. The need for grandparents and all their children's families to work as a large family unit no longer exists. The role of the grandparents has changed from being a needed, integral part of the pioneer family and the slave community to being rarely relied upon by today's family.

The family units have become smaller. The work of the large majority of fathers has changed from farming, hunting, and fishing to employment in an urbanized community. Most mothers find their situation changed from that of being solely responsible for the family's clothing, food, and education (in many instances) to reliance on schools, manufacturers, farmers, and stores for her family's needs. The cost of supplying all these services and products has been an influence on many women to accept employment outside the family unit. Many have become economically independent. Divorce has become more prevalent as women have become more independent and have gained more rights.

Today's children have more responsibilities in becoming educated and fewer tasks to perform in the home than those who were a part of the self-sufficient pioneer family.

Life begins with life

At the age of nine, most children have grasped the idea that life begins with life. The teacher, however, cannot assume that all children understand this, so she must provide experiences that teach or strengthen previous learning.

One way to approach the goal of teaching that life can only come from life is to have a study of cells, which most nine-year-old children find fascinating. Through this study, children will be able to learn that all living organisms are made up of cells and that new life begins with cells from the parent organisms. These cells multiply, and in this way new plant and animal life are created and grown. The process of creating new life is called reproduction. All types of life must reproduce themselves, if they are to continue to exist.

Learning about plant cells

Experiments can be conducted by viewing plant cells under the microscope. Some classrooms have very simple, inexpensive microscopes for each child. A micro-projector is a type of microscope many schools use. This makes it possible for the whole class to view the cell slide at the same time, since it projects the picture onto a screen. If the classroom has only one or two individual microscopes, the study can still be undertaken successfully with an extra bit of teacher planning.

One of the simplest cells to view is an onion-skin cell. Cut off a thin piece of onion, and then peel from that the thinnest possible bit of skin. Place this on a slide and view. If a cover slip is used, add a drop of water to the skin before covering. Children can easily see the rectangular cells.

To see the nucleus in each cell, repeat this experiment with a stain made of half water and half iodine. One drop of stain placed on the onion skin from the end of a toothpick and allowed to set for about five minutes will make the nucleus in each cell visible. Skin specimens from other parts of the onion should also be studied. Make certain that each child understands that the onion is made completely of cells, and that each cell has a nucleus. Point out that all living organisms are made of cells—not only the onion. Also, help the children recognize that the single cell is the smallest particle of all living matter.

To help children see the cells of a different plant, a leaf from the aquarium plant Elodea may be used. One recommended way for children to prepare the slide is to warm it in lukewarm water. Then place a leaf in the center, add a drop of lukewarm water, and put on a cover slip. When children study the specimen through the microscope, they should be able to see chloroplasts (green chlorophyll bodies) moving slowly inside each cell. This is protoplasm moving inside the cell. The cell membrane, the nucleus, and the cytoplasm are made of a material called protoplasm. Protoplasm is a term for the material which has the properties of life and from which all living things are made.

Chromosomes and genes

The children cannot see the chromosomes and genes inside the nucleus, but they can understand their presence and function if they are told about them.

TEACHER: *Isn't the cell tiny? It is good that we have a microscope which enlarges it many, many times, so that we can see it.*

CHILD: *It sure is little. It's the littlest part of the organism.*

TEACHER: *We also found something very tiny in each cell. Who remembers what it's called?*

CHILD: *I know. It's the nucleus.*

TEACHER: *Good for you! You remembered the name for that part. It's called the nucleus. The nucleus is somewhat like the boss of the cell, it controls the activities of the cell. Now I'm going to tell you about something even more amazing. It sounds like magic, and it's hard to believe because it's so fantastic. Inside of each nucleus are many tiny threadlike objects called chromosomes.*

CHILD: *In that little thing? Hey, I can't see any little threads.*

TEACHER: *No, you can't see them, but they are there. Something even more fantastic is there. On each chromosome are still smaller particles called genes. These genes decide the characteristics that the organism inherits from the parent organism. That is why the cells of an Elodea plant go on reproducing Elodea plants, and the cells of people go on reproducing people.*

CHILD: *I get it. The genes are really the big boss that tells what the new cells will be.*

TEACHER: *Right. What would happen if we could remove the nucleus of a cell?*

CHILD: *If the nucleus wasn't there, then the chromo-*

somes and genes wouldn't be there, and then the cell wouldn't be able to make a new cell.

TEACHER: You figured that out very well. Genes are very important to you, too. Is there something about you that someone has said you inherited from your father or mother or grandparents?

CHILD: Everybody says I look like my mother, and that our noses are just the same.

TEACHER: The genes did that. They determined the kind of nose you would have.

CHILD: I have blue eyes like my mom and dad.

TEACHER: The genes were responsible for that.

CHILD: My grandmother says I look like my mother and my father.

TEACHER: You inherited half your genes from your mother and her family, and half from your father and his family, so you inherited characteristics from each.

Seeing living cells and blood circulation

Another experiment that children find exciting and meaningful is to observe the living cells and circulating blood of a goldfish. This specimen is particularly well suited for the microprojector, where all children can see the circulation and cells at the same time.

Wrap the body of the goldfish carefully in wet cotton, leaving the tail exposed. Focus the microscope on the tail. A slide may be placed over the tail to keep it still. The children, of course, will be concerned that this may harm the fish, so assure them prior to the viewing that the fish will be fine when returned to the water. The observation time should of necessity be short.

Protozoa

Children armed with a microscope discover that hunting for one-celled animals is exciting. These one-celled primitive animals belong to a group called Protozoa. They sometimes form colonies, but each cell continues to function as if it were a single organism.

Most protozoa, such as amoebas and paramecia, reproduce by dividing in two. This process is called fission. This is asexual reproduction, since the organism reproduces itself as only one parent with no sexual organs. The dividing cell, however, is called the parent until it separates. The two separate one-celled animals are then called daughter cells. These daughter cells in turn develop into parent cells and then divide. The nucleus divides with the rest of the cell, and in this way each cell has a nucleus. Some protozoa reproduce by multiple fission, reproducing more than two offspring at a time. This method is called sporulation.

A few protozoa reproduce by budding. In these protozoa a bud develops and grows larger. Then it breaks off, and becomes a new organism. It, too, will have a nucleus from the parent cell.

To see these one-celled animals that take in food, digest it, throw away the wastes, move about, breathe, and grow, cultures may be prepared that encourage growth of protozoa. A culture can be made with hay, dried grass, or dried lettuce and put loosely into a jar that is then filled with water. Cover the jar with cheesecloth held in place with a rubberband. Put the jar into a dark closet for about two weeks. Then examine drops of the culture under the microscope.

Another interesting culture can be made by collecting pond water. Fill five-gallon jars half-full of pond water. In one jar drop crumbled pieces of yolk from a hard-boiled egg. In the second jar drop five or six grains of rice. In the third jar put five or six grains of wheat. Put no food into the fourth and fifth jars. Store the jars where they will not get too warm or receive too much light. Observe the five jars carefully for a week or two, to see if tiny specks can be seen swimming about. Discover if the jars with the egg yolk and grains have more specks than those with plain pond water. The decay bacteria and small protozoa are used for food by larger protozoa.

Using the microscope to examine drops of water from the cultures is an exciting adventure for children. If a child discovers a protozoan dividing, the edges of the cover slip can be sealed with vaseline to prevent the water from evaporating. If the slide dries out, the cells will die. Encourage the children to draw what they see through the microscope.

Letting children see pictures of the amoeba and the paramecium will help them to identify the life they find in their drop of pond water as they examine it under the microscope. Transparencies, *Science #3-Biology* pp. 63–64, "Amoeba" and "Paramecia," by the 3M Company, give children a good chance to study the cells.

More cells

Seeing cells from their own body can be achieved by having the children rub their cheek linings gently with the broad end of a toothpick or tongue depressor. Gently deposit the material gathered on the toothpick onto a slide. Again a drop of iodine diluted with water will be an effective stain to help children see their own cells.

Children will think of other sources for gathering cells to view: dead skin that peels off after a sunburn, the skin of a chameleon when he molts, and algae from the fish tank are but a few.

Help children see that the cells of all the specimens they have viewed are close to the same size. The cells from a child's cheek are about the same size as the cells of the small, thin peel of onion. Also, the cells are not larger in a big person or smaller in a small person. They are simply more numerous.

TEACHER: We talked about the size of cells and decided that a human being's cells and an onion's cells are about—what size?

CHILD: About the same size, and they are all very, very small.

TEACHER: Right! If the cells are about the same size, then how does it happen that a person is much bigger than an onion?

CHILD: Because people have lots more cells.

TEACHER: Yes, people have many, many more cells. Can you estimate how many cells it would take to make you?

CHILD: It would take thousands and thousands.

TEACHER: More than that.

CHILD: Millions and millions?

TEACHER: More than that.

CHILD: Billions?

TEACHER: Even more.

CHILD: Trillions?

TEACHER: That sounds more like it! What is our skin made of?

CHILDREN: Cells!

TEACHER: What are our eyes made of?

CHILDREN: Cells!

TEACHER: And our muscles?

CHILDREN: Cells!

TEACHER: Yes, every part of us is made of cells. What do these cells do for us?

CHILD: They keep us alive, and make new cells. That's why I'm growing bigger.

TEACHER: You're right. Does a cell ever die?

CHILD: I don't think so, 'cause then we would die.

TEACHER: Are you sure? Suppose you fall down in the playground and skin your knees—what happens that makes the hurt?

CHILD: The skin got scraped off.

TEACHER: The skin that is destroyed was made of cells, so the cells are destroyed. If they are destroyed are they dead or alive?

CHILD: They're dead.

TEACHER: Will you die because some cells died?
CHILD: No, of course not.
TEACHER: Right. So if a few cells die, you don't die with them. Many cells wear out and die. What must the living cells do about the dead cells?
CHILD: Make new cells. They must reproduce.
TEACHER: How do cells reproduce?
CHILD: They divide.
TEACHER: Yes, most of the cells reproduce by dividing. When they divide each part must have something special. What is it?
CHILD: Protoplasm?
TEACHER: Yes, but one thing each living cell must have is—?
CHILD: A nucleus!
TEACHER: Right! When a cell divides, the nucleus must divide, too, so each cell will have a nucleus.

The teacher can help the children learn that cells of the same kind cluster together to make tissues. These special tissues in a human being made the various parts of the eye, the heart, muscles, bone, skin, nerves, brains, liver, kidneys, and all the many parts of the body. Each cell reproduces more cells of its own kind to carry on its specialized function.

Reproduction cells

The children may recall that the female reproductive cell is called an egg cell or ovum, while the male reproductive cell is called the sperm cell. If children do not bring it into the cell study, the teacher may help them to remember that all animal life begins when the ovum and sperm unite.

TEACHER: You learned about how animals and people reproduce. Who can tell us how each new life starts?
CHILD: I know. An egg cell!
TEACHER: Good for you! That's right. The egg or

ovum is a tiny cell. But it isn't a complete cell, and it can't break apart and start a new cell. Does anyone know why?
CHILD: *It needs to have a sperm cell join it. Then it's a complete cell, and a baby begins to grow.*
TEACHER: *Yes, when a male sperm cell unites with a female egg cell, it is a complete cell. Then it can divide and divide and divide until there are millions of cells and a new life has been reproduced.*

Other living animals

If other living animals are included in the science unit for children of this age, special care should be taken to incorporate the reproduction of each animal as a part of the study. Many books and curriculums have been written giving children a fine introduction to understanding animals and their usefulness to man, but rarely do they include the miraculous and complete ways in which these animals reproduce. All living things would become extinct if it were not for reproduction. Why should this all-important phase be excluded and ignored in an animal study? In the past, if reproduction was introduced in the classroom, credit was given solely to the female sex for the miracle of birth.

Children who learn about cells and the division of cells marvel at the unique way in which a complete cell is formed to start a new life. This fact makes the miraculous reproduction cell different from all other cells, and the most important cell of all!

Throughout the elementary school, sex education is usually best taught by relating it to regular classroom studies rather than as a separate subject. This places the responsibility upon the teacher to recognize the appropriate times to teach about the family, the reproduction process of all living organisms (including human beings), how our own sexuality affects each of us, our responsibilities to others, and respect for ourselves and others.

Morals and appreciation cannot be taught as separate subjects, but the teacher's keen interest, understanding, awe, and respect for people and the world we live in are caught by the children as she teaches.

Chapter Eleven

The Preadolescent at Home

Behavior characteristics

Childhood is coming to an end and adolescence is nearing. Parents are often jolted into awareness of the impending change by small, isolated suggestions: Jack looks different, Mary is growing a few hairs in her armpits, Jean is sure she needs a bra because of two small pimple-like projections on her chest, Mark is getting moody spells, and Carol's temper flares up without provocation. What is happening? Most parents are completely unprepared psychologically for this age, for it always seems to arrive too quickly. What has happened to their predictable son and their cooperative daughter? They have reached "that age"! Bodily changes are beginnning to take place, which also changes the feelings inside of them. The children are much more perplexed by these new feelings and behavior than their parents.

When does this begin? Any time between ten and thirteen, and it may occur at nine for a few children and later than thirteen for others. The timetable of maturation is not the same for all.

Behavior at ten

At ten, many children accept life and all its ups and downs with easygoing aplomb. They like their home and insist on being a part of everything that is going on when they are with the family. They seem to be constantly under foot and incessantly talking; they rarely stay in their rooms to read or play.

Ten has high ideals and is usually strongly against cheating, smoking, drunkenness, narcotics and other evils they read and hear about. They want to be good children and to be successful at school, but they also do not want to outrank their friends. They like the thought of being comfortably wedged into the class average of performance and ability.

Boys still prefer playing with boys and particularly enjoy groups of boys. A good game of baseball usually is tops in their list of fun activities. Most boys candidly express disinterest in girls, and a few actively dislike them. Girls usually play with girls, but prefer small groups. They easily get "mad" at a friend and will exclude her from the group for a short while.

A few girls this age become interested in boys and try to get their attention. One girl told her mother she was no longer going "steady" with Joe. The mother hid her surprise at her daughter's announcement, for she had not been aware that her child had had anything at all to do with the boy. She asked in a sympathetic voice about the cause of the breakup. As the daughter told the whole story, the mother was able to discern that "going steady" meant the boy liked her daughter. The young admirer had slipped a note to her at school which read, "You are pretty. Will you go steady with me? Love, Joe." Beyond passing a few notes of mutual admiration, the "going steady" had no significance.

Ten is an active child, and sitting in a chair soon becomes an acrobatic feat. His room is messy and he delares that he likes it best that way. The easiest way to cope with ten's mess is to ignore it and keep the door closed; however, insisting that he has occasional room-cleaning sessions is not ony a necessity, but valuable for him to learn. Many teens resist baths, even though they have taken daily baths up to that age. They always seem to have dirty hands and faces, and only reach for the soap to keep mother from "blowing her top." Many boys feel as strongly about combing their hair as they do about soap and water. They usually want their hair cut (or not cut) according to the prevailing styles, but then completely neglect it. If teased about their dirty, uncombed hair, they often good-naturedly reach up with both hands and do a thorough job of stirring it up. They then ask with a laugh, "How's this?"

Ten and sex

Girls at this age are less concerned about babies and how they develop, and more interested in themselves. This is particularly true of the girl who is starting sexual development.

Menstruation in particular interests them, and they want to know all there is to know about the subject. Most girls do not menstruate before eleven, but there are a few who start at ten or even nine.

Boys seldom show bodily changes at ten, and are less interested than girls in their own sex growth. Most boys know about intercourse (whether told by parents or not) and express interest in the father's role. They are intrigued by the growth of a baby and want to see books that show pictures of the fetus.

Tens—particularly boys—often use "dirty words"

about elimination or sex, and when asked what these words mean they are unable to explain.

Behavior at eleven

Eleven-year-olds like to talk, eat, and argue. Their emotional life is at a high pitch, and they can fly into a rage over the slightest thing. Eleven is cheerful one minute and moody the next. He is often very critical of his parents (the same parents who were so perfect a short time ago) and finds fault with almost everything about them.

"Dad, when my friends come over, please don't try to be funny!" or "Good grief, Mom, you aren't going to wear that dopey dress to the Scout Parents' Night!" are typical of the jolts given parents by their eleven-year-olds. If parents return their fire, they may receive a dramatic performance that makes a guillotine scene seem mild by contrast. Girls often open the reservoir, and tears cascade down their faces. Added to this will be sobbed protests, "Everyone hates me! You don't care how you hurt me!" At this point they may dramatically flounce out of the room to seek a haven elsewhere. Boys often meet parents' criticism with insolence. If not checked, they will enjoy the dramatic effect so much that they will increase their brash, name-calling rebellion and become downright obnoxious.

If a youngster is heaping his wrath on Mother, Father can step into the scene and say firmly, "Now see here, Tom, we know you are hopping mad, but that is no reason for you to take it out on your mother. I will not allow you to talk to my wife in this manner. When you have calmed down, your mother and I will be happy to try to find a solution that will satisfy you and us."

Elevens are not always in the throes of anger, hurt feelings, and moodiness, for they also have their high, gay moods along with flashes of affection.

The heightened activity of ten increases at eleven. Sitting in a chair is even more difficult. Eleven rocks, jerks, bounces, hops up and then throws himself back in the chair, dangles legs over the arms, and then thumps back onto the floor. Along with all these movements, eleven's hands and arms are also in constant motion, pulling up socks, fiddling with shoes, cracking knuckles, and picking at cuticle. As if not to be outdone, the face joins the symphony and eyebrows go up and down, lips are pursed and then stretched in a grin, the nose sniffs and wrinkles, and some children can even wiggle their ears. This incessant bodily movement seems to be the result of inner churning and changing.

Eleven's extremes are even manifested in his choice of foods. He either dearly loves a type of food or abhors it.

Eleven is more underfoot in the home than when he was ten. If he has homework, he wants to do it right in the family circle. He seems to forget that he has a room and seldom goes to it except to sleep. This age may also be more fearful than younger ages, a fearfulness perhaps in part caused by his morbid interest in all the crime reported in the newspapers and on radio and TV. To add to the frightening aspects of a murder or kidnapping that has occurred somewhere, eleven and his peers seem to delight in discussing all the gory details and creating a few more hair-raising items to add to the case. When most elevens go to bed at night, they betray their fears by checking closets and looking under the bed, just for safety. They also like a hall light on and their door ajar. A flashlight is often next to their bed, in case the electricity goes off for some reason.

A child this age may keep himself awake at night with fantasies of sudden fame and riches, or being the hero of some great adventure. When morning arrives, these heroes seem so drugged by sleep that they can barely get out of bed. They usually arrive late at the breakfast table, under their own little black, ominous cloud. It seems wise to let a child this age eat breakfast alone, while the rest of the household tries to avoid open conflicts with him.

Boys still enjoy being part of a group of boys (or a gang, as they usually refer to it), but they are learning to be more discriminating about the friends they choose. Many boys now choose to have a best friend they can rely upon, and enjoy spending the night at each other's home.

Girls usually are with a small group of girls, and they, too, like to spend the night at each other's home. It is even more interesting if it becomes a slumber party of four or five girls. Their main topic of conversation at these parties is boys.

Eleven and sex

A small number of eleven-year-old girls have the rounded contours and physical sexual growth of an adolescent. At the other end of the growth pattern are some girls who show no trace of sexual development. The vast majority of eleven-year-old girls, however, are following the average development pattern. By the end of the year most of them have lost the straight figure of a child and are becoming more feminine in appearance. Their hips are broadening and growing more curved, while their waists appear to have narrowed. Their breasts are developing into small mounds, and many now wear the bras they yearned for at an earlier age. Most of them have pubic hair. The height growth has accelerated for most, and many have reached roughly 90 per cent of their adult height.

The eleven-year-old girl is so involved in watching her own sexual development that she has little interest in other aspects of sex. She is often curious about boys and wonders if they go through a growth change also. If she has an adult with whom she feels comfortable in talking about personal things, she will undoubtedly seek the answer there; otherwise she must rely on information her friends can give her.

Boys' sexual development comes later than the girls'. Most boys show practically no outward signs at eleven years of age. There is, however, an increase in bone size in many boys. Some boys have a "fat period" at this time, which many find embarrassing, since the excess layers of fat choose the hips and chest on which to settle. Some boys' breasts enlarge to such a degree that they refuse to go swimming or undress in front of other boys. Height growth in boys is not accelerated at this time as it is with many girls, and boys often find themselves shorter than the girls their age. This fact usually does not disturb either the boys or girls.

A small number of boys will show beginning sexual changes at eleven and start an acceleration of height growth. At the other extreme are a small group of boys who show no change, not even bone enlargement, and who seem less masculine than their peers. Special reassurances should be given these small boys, for they often fear that they will never grow to be real men. These slow-growing little boys often turn out to be taller and more masculine adults than those who mature early.

Behavior at twelve

The twelve-year-old is in the early stages of adolescence. He is less of a chatterbox and gives evidence of becoming introspective and even self-critical. His emotions are under control most of the time; however, he can quickly lose this control if he feels he is being regarded as a baby. Twelve wants to be treated as an adult, albeit he does not always deserve it. Parents may be showered with sudden anger and tears if they make the grievous error of demanding childlike obedience.

One school morning, a twelve-year-old girl came flying down the stairs, late as usual, grabbed her books and started out of the door with a cheery, "Bye, Mum."

MOTHER: *Lynne, come back here. You haven't eaten your breakfast.*

LYNNE: *Haven't time, Mum. I'm late.*

MOTHER: *You come right back and sit down and drink that milk at least!*

LYNNE: *Oh, Mothe-e-e-r, I haven't time! Anyway, my stomach feels funny and I'll vomit if I drink that junk!*

MOTHER: *You heard me! Come back here! You'll drink that milk, if I have to pour it down your throat! No daughter of mine is going to school without breakfast!*

Going to school angry and in tears (with milk in the stomach) is more harmful than going to school without breakfast. The mother was right in insisting that breakfast is necessary for a growing child, but peaceful solutions can be found. To begin with, suggestions are better than demands. If Lynne really has no time for breakfast, it would be more helpful to let her go this one time. In the evening, mother and daughter could calmly discuss what problem makes her so late. The mother could at this time help her daughter understand why she feels that breakfast is an important meal and is not to be skipped. The chances are good that it may never happen again, and the confrontation can be avoided.

Twelve is becoming more and more aware of his peers. He wants friends near him all the time, but shows more selectiveness in choosing his favorite friends. It is important to him that he look and act like all the others in his age group. They are so aware of wanting to be one of the gang that they often dress as though their clothes all came from the same model. Wheat jeans, blue jeans, babushkas, saddle shoes, sneakers, curly hair, straight hair, long skirts, slacks, short skirts, and trench coats have all had their wave of popularity with adolescents. How these styles get so throughly entrenched is hard to determine, but the group leaders wear and like them, and soon every adolescent in the country blends into the pattern. There is safety for the individual when he is surrounded by carbon copies.

One father drove his daughter and several of her friends to junior high school one rainy morning. When he stopped at the school, the girls ran to the waiting crowd of children. Girls were massed on one side of the entrance and boys on the other. The father's daughter and her friends melted into the swaying expanse of raincoated forms (all beige-colored coats with babushkas covering the hair, the style that year). He had the strange feeling that he might never see his daughter again, for she became indistinguishable in the crowd.

Twelve goes back to bathing once again and usually brushes his teeth without being told. Many girls are very particular about their hair style, but may forget to clean their nails and wash their ears.

Twelve is a collector of mementoes, ticket stubs from a movie, pennants, pictures of friends, autographed pictures of current entertainment idols, notes passed at school, postcards, party favors, and other such memorabilia. Bulletin boards or scrapbooks are needed at this age to hold the endless collections.

Twelve is clever at saving money out of his allowance so he will have ready cash in case his friends want to do something special that costs money. He will save bus fare by walking to school and buying less for lunch, thus filling his kitty. Some twelves are so eager for money that they become quite ingenious in thinking up ways to earn it.

Stealing is quite prevalent at this age. Girls succumb

to shop-lifting more often than boys. If these children are caught right on the spot, it often results in an instant cure. The child who is not caught may try it again and again. The child's peers are usually the first to learn about the stealing. If the school is told, the parents should be informed. Parents are often the last to hear about their child's problem. The school and home should communicate with each other, for they have the common goal of wanting what is best for the child. Children who are caught, and helped to understand that it is unacceptable, usually do not continue stealing.

Twelve and sex

The majority of girls make their most rapid growth in height and weight during this year, and many girls have gained 95 per cent of their full height by the end of the twelfth year. Their breasts fill out, and most girls examine them daily to check on their growth. Many times one breast grows larger than the other, and the child must be assured that this is normal and common.

Underarm hair begins to grow, and twelve needs her mother's instruction on how safely to shave the hair. A mild deodorant may also be needed, for children this age often begin to perspire heavily in the armpits. Mothers should advise their daughters and sons also, on the necessity of cleanliness. Not only is a daily bath needed, but fresh underclothes, too. Many girls begin to menstruate sometime during the twelfth year. They should be fully informed about menstruation and have the necessary equipment ready in the event that it begins. If a girl understands the reason for her periods and knows what to expect, she normally looks forward to it. These girls are sure that menstruation proves them to be adults. Mothers need to help their daughters learn how to fasten a sanitary pad, how and where to dispose of it, and the necessity of changing the pad several times a day; they need to understand the importance of fastidious care.

Some twelve-year-old girls will continue to have little-girl shapes, with no visible signs of sexual maturing. They need reassuring that they, too, will change and that growth patterns vary among all people. Many of these girls beg to have a padded bra, so that they may feel and look more like the average twelve-year-old.

Boys have a wide variation of maturity at this age. On the whole, boys mature about a year later than girls. However, the twelfth year brings definite signs of the beginning of puberty for many boys. They will have increased growth of the penis and scrotum, and a bit of pubic hair will grow. A boy's interest in sex now begins to turn to himself. He may check to see if his penis is growing as fast as other boys'. The boys who are not maturing are often teased by those who are. Adults must help these boys who mature more slowly to be patient and to know that they, too, will reach that stage in life.

Erections of the penis often occur at this age but are seldom sexually motivated. A full bladder, exercise, reading, or excitement are among the causes for erection. It is a perfectly normal happening. Boys who have reached puberty may have seminal emissions (wet dreams). If a child has not been forewarned, this may disturb him greatly. When a mother detects a stain on the sheets or pajamas and has not spoken to her son about it previously, she must do so now.

MOTHER: *I noticed a stain on your sheet. You probably had a seminal emission. Some people call them wet dreams. Were you aware of it?*
SON: *Yeah, I guess so.*
MOTHER: *Dad or I should have told you about it a long*

time ago. I guess we just can't believe you're getting as old as you are. Seminal emission is just another sign of your growing up.

SON: Yeah?

MOTHER: Sperm cells and semen develop in the testes when boys mature. Occasionally the testes are so filled that some will come out. This usually happens during sleep. That's why some people call it a wet dream.

SON: I heard some kids talk about wet dreams, but I didn't know they meant this. You know, I thought maybe I was going back to a baby habit, and that I wet my bed a little bit. Wouldn't that be crazy!

MOTHER: I'm not so sure I'd like to have you go back to that habit. I remember those daily washes I had when all my children were babies. By the way, the next time you have a seminal emission you may want to change into a fresh pair of pajamas. If you think of something I haven't explained, be sure to ask.

Oftentimes parents decide that the father should talk to his son about sexual maturity; but, when parents and children are in the habit of talking about anything that concerns children, parents, and family, either parent may speak to a child of either sex. This close, relaxed relationship between parent and child helps the child to feel free to go to either parent for help and advice.

Some boys do not have seminal emissions, which is also considered normal. A boy must know that many or few or no seminal emissions are all considered normal. Old wives' tales such as "A boy's manliness is escaping during seminal emissions," are sometimes passed from boy to boy. These notions are false and boys must be told.

Both boys and girls must again be warned about sex deviates. Boys face the possibility of being seduced by an older male for sex play. They should be fully informed and understand that the person may be a teenager or an old man, he may be a derelict or a respected citizen. The child should not be frightened by your advice, but rather informed, so he will know how to protect himself.

Some boys or girls will have one homosexual experience at this age. Usually it is not repeated. If a parent discovers that it has happened more often, he must speak frankly to his child about it. If the cause is an undesirable friend, he must be helped to see that the boy or girl is not acting normally, and needs help. In the meantime, he must stop his association and find other friends. The parent should not make his child feel guilty or "dirty" because of his actions, but rather help him learn that it is undesirable and immature to enter into this kind of activity.

Parents' behavior

How do parents cope with this new child, this pre-adolescent child they suddenly have on their hands? One father, after a particularly stormy weekend, suggested to his exhausted wife, "Why don't we just lock Amy in a closet and let her out in several years when she's over this awful age!"

If parents become thoroughly informed about the many physical changes that are occurring in this child, they may better understand the inner seething that takes place. A sense of humor helps many a parent over this hurdle. Patience and a mature attitude are two other necessary traits needed to help the parents in dealing with their child. When an adult screams, cries, and strikes out at the preadolescent, he is being as immature and confused as the child. Many storms can be avoided by overlooking all minor (although irritating) mistakes or actions. Eleven simply cannot handle constant criticism hurled his way, and the sooner a parent understands this the better it will be for all involved. Keep the criticisms for some really big, important problems. Remembering that this age will pass, and that with time there will come a calmer, more mature child, is comforting to the concerned parents.

Parent-and-child "fights" make it almost impossible for a child to regard his parent as an ally. The parent who demands that his child do his bidding at the moment he has decreed will discover that his ultimatum turns out to be a declaration of war. To the changing and confused child, an adult's dictatorial manner is intolerable and insulting to a person of his stature. He no longer feels like a little child, and he wants adults to know it. He of course also realizes that he is not an adult. The fact is, he is not sure just where he fits. He wants adult treatment, but not necessarily adult responsibility. His inconsistencies annoy many parents, but how else will he learn? He cannot suddenly change from small child to adult. He needs to fumble along trying out this and that role, and eventually choose what is right for him. Guidance, love, and family traditions and values do influence children as they grow to adulthood, even though many parents declare that they see no evidence of it during the transitional years.

There are times when parents feel that the pre-adolescent and adolescent child has built a strong brick wall between them and himself, but there are many times when a parent can go gently around or over that not-so-formidable hurdle. A parent should rejoice each time his child comes to him with problems or for advice. These are the moments when a receptive listener and a compassionate adviser makes the difference between building the wall higher or taking down some of the bricks.

Puzzled parents

A sweet, cooperative, and loving child can have sudden moments of boorish behavior. This is more noticeable in girls than in boys.

"What's wrong with Lisa?" asked a puzzled father after being rudely rebuffed by his eleven-year-old daughter.

"Why, what did she do?" inquired his wife, almost dreading to hear.

"When I came in just now, I had to gingerly step around Lisa and friends who were sprawled all over the steps," explained the father. "My 'Hello, girls,' which I said in my cheeriest voice (in spite of their rudeness in not moving), was met with stony silence and blank looks. As I stepped around Lisa, I gave her a quick hello kiss on the top of her head. She jumped up as though I had kicked her and snarled in her nastiest voice, 'Oh, for Pete's sake, Dad!' It took all the willpower I had not to give her a good slap across the mouth!"

"By now, I'm sure she realizes how rude she was," soothed his wife. "And I'm glad that you ignored her nastiness. Later we can talk to her, if she doesn't apologize. These unexpected personality changes are happening more and more. It must indicate that Lisa feels pretty mixed-up. It's preadolescence, I suppose," she sighed.

Liza did not apologize and pretended nothing had happened. That evening, when she was ready for bed, she gave a goodnight kiss to her mother and then to her father. Her father said kindly, with a hint of humor, "I'm glad I got a goodnight kiss. I've been worrying that you wouldn't give me one."

"Aw Dad, I like to kiss you, but not outside," answered Lisa. "It's babyish to kiss Mommy and Daddy where everyone can see. I'll bet the kids thought it was corny," she added.

"That's strange," commented the mother, "I like it when Dad gives me a hello kiss, whether I'm outside or in."

"Aw, that's different, you're his wife," explained Lisa.

"Oh, I see," said the father, in spite of being baffled at the distinction. "If you don't want me to kiss you outdoors, I'll remember to skip you." Then he added with a twinkle, "Is it okay if I say, 'Hi'?"

"Aw Dad, stop teasing me," answered Lisa, "I guess it wasn't very nice of me to yell at you this afternoon. I'm sorry."

Another parent-deflating preadolescent jolt is the frank announcement that the child prefers friends to parents for a social occasion. One hot summer day a father noted on the neighborhood theater marquee that a movie he wanted to see was being shown that night. When he came home from work, his suggestion to go to the movies was accepted with delight by his wife but rejected by his daughter.

"What's the matter, honey, do you have other plans? If you do, we can go tomorrow night," offered the father.

"No, I just don't want to go," his daughter answered testily.

"But you said the other night you wanted to see this movie," he reminded her. "What changed your mind?"

"Nobody my age goes to the movies with their family. That's for babies!" she sniffed haughtily.

"Don't be ridiculous! I see plenty of kids with their parents, and besides, babies don't go to the movies. What's wrong with you? Do you think you're too good to go to the movies with your parents?" asked the ruffled father.

"I said I don't want to go," came the stubborn answer. "Kids my age go to the movies with their friends, not with their parents. It's embarrassing!"

"Well, I've got news for you! You're going whether you like it or not," sputtered her father.

And she went! With a resigned expression and in haughty silence she followed her parents, at a discreet distance, into the theater. She hoped that no one would guess that she, at her age, was going with her parents to the movies! Later the adults decided it had not been worth the effort to prove that their daughter's stubbornness was foolish.

"Maybe I was the foolish one," the father admitted, "You know, I do believe my nose was out of joint because my one and only child chose her silly friends instead of me."

Forming attitudes toward sex

In a home where each person is accepted lovingly as he is, despite any present annoying problems, the communication lines usually do not close down entirely. Questions about sex will be eliminated by the child, however, if he feels that his parents are embarrassed to answer them. The adult's discomfort increases the child's insecurity in approaching the subject. There must be no subject too difficult to discuss in the privacy of the home. Parents' lack of knowledge is understandable and accepted by children; however, they do expect adults to know how to find the answers.

Parent and child sharing a book such as *Wonderfully Made* or *Human Reproduction** will give them a basis on which to have conversations about growing up. These books have been written specifically for children approaching or beginning adolescence.

A child's attitude about his body, his sexuality, and sex in general is slowly formed as he adds bit after bit of information. Whether the attitudes he forms will be wholesome, appreciative, and respectful or whether they will be unappreciative and lacking in respect and moral feeling depends on how and where he receives this information.

All too often the home, church, and school have failed the child in this area of education and have left these all-important learnings to haphazard seeking on the part of the youth. Yet, strangely enough, exemplary results are expected when he reaches adulthood.

A child who must seek his information from his peers or from magazines and books he reads by chance, has little occasion to build respectful and wholesome attitudes.

He can be given a realistic opportunity to gain the right attitudes and morals if his home provides the foundation on which he can build sound values, while the church adds to his dimension of understanding by helping him to learn God's plan for man, and the school supplements the teaching of home and church.

Home and school encourage learning

Liz was ten years old and in Mrs. Evans' fifth-grade class. The children were studying the body systems, and each evening at the dinner table Liz would tell her parents some interesting facts she had learned that day.

LIZ: *Do you know that man has never invented a kidney machine that works as successfully as the little kidneys in our body? Isn't that amazing?*

FATHER: *That's very interesting. What do the kidneys do for us?*

LIZ: *Why, they're the body's filtration system. They filter out all the waste materials picked up by our blood. If they stopped working, we'd be poisoned and die.*

FATHER: *It seems to me I read that a machine has been invented to do the work of the kidneys.*

LIZ: *There is a machine, Mrs. Evans said. In fact, she had a picture of a man lying in bed using the machine. It takes all night for the machine to take out the wastes, and the man has to be connected to the machine several times a week. The machine is very expensive, and takes a long time to do the work. And there aren't enough machines to help all the people in the world who need them.*

FATHER: *Well, healthy kidneys sound mighty important. It's amazing that those little organs can function all our life without our even being aware of them, and they are doing their job while we sleep and while we work. I feel very, very thankful I have them.*

LIZ: *Isn't it amazing! Our bodies are filled with unbelievable organs and things.*

The family looked forward to their discussions about the body systems. The reproductive system was also studied, along with the digestive system, the circulatory system, and the nervous system. Liz's teacher had made the study an exciting one, and the children were gaining a good understanding of the systems and a deep appreciation for them.

LIZ: *We're going to have fun at school. Mrs. Evans is helping us plan a sort of contest. We kids divided up into groups, and each group will gather all the evidence possible on why the body system we chose to work on is the most important one of all. I had a hard time deciding which system to work on.*

MOTHER: *Well, which one did you choose?*

LIZ: *The reproduction system. Tomorrow we all start finding facts which will prove how important the system we chose really is.*

MOTHER: *You already know a good deal about reproduction.*

LIZ: *Yes, but not enough to have our group win.*

FATHER: *Who will decide if you win or lose?*

LIZ: *That's the fun part. We're going to make posters and diagrams and pictures and stuff for an exhibit. We also have to tell about it. Mrs. Evans said that she can tell we will be mighty busy the next few days. When we're ready, we're going to present our evidence to the jury and judge, who'll decide which is most important.*

MOTHER: *Who will the jury be?*

LIZ: *We are going to ask the sixth grade to be the jury and Mr. White [the principal] to be the judge.*

The verdict of the sixth-grade jury, after hearing and seeing all the evidence, was that each body system was the most important.

That night, after Liz recounted all the details of the contest and the jury's decision, the father added to the grace at table, "And thank you, God, for the wonderful bodies we have. As your children, we will each nourish and care for our bodies."

Questions asked of parents

Questions asked of parents about sex or any other subject usually are popped at them unexpectedly. "Is it true that cookies make a person fat?" or "What are wisdom teeth for?" or "Do you think I'll start menstruating soon?" As a child's thoughts flit from subject to subject, he suddenly becomes curious about one thing or another. Quick, simple answers usually satisfy.

CHILD: *If I start to menstruate the first time in school, what should I do?*

MOTHER: *Ask to go to the lavatory, and then check your panties. If there is a drop of blood on them, then you have started. Does the lavatory have machines with sanitary napkins?*

CHILD: *No, but our teacher told us we can get one from the school nurse or the school secretary.*

MOTHER: *Well, then ask your teacher if you may go to see the nurse.*

CHILD: *But what if she says no? I can't tell her I'm sick. That would be a lie.*

MOTHER: *You must tell her that you have started to menstruate and need to see the nurse or secretary. She'll let you go.*

Reading the newspapers brings crimes and murders and news of sex crimes to children at an early age. Ten-year-old Jim read that a girl had been kidnapped and raped.

J I M : Mom, what's raped?

M O T H E R : What are you reading, Jim?

J I M : Well, it says that a girl was kidnapped by a man and taken to a field and raped.

M O T H E R : It means that the man took the girl by force, against her will, and then mistreated her.

J I M : You mean he hit her?

M O T H E R : No, raped means to force the sexual act upon her. Men who do this are mentally sick and are sometimes called "sex morons." These men force their penis into the girl's vagina for their own sick pleasure. It is a sinful and dreadful thing for a man to rape a girl or woman. Think how frightened the poor girl must have been. Sometimes these mentally sick people even kill the girls so they can't tell who did it.

J I M : Gosh, I hope the police catch that man. They ought to kill him.

M O T H E R : I hope they catch him, so he can't hurt some other girl. Perhaps doctors can help his sick mind.

Children who have been told from babyhood on that a baby begins when a sperm cell from the father joins and unites with an egg cell from the mother may never have questioned how these cells got to each other. They may have been given this information, but that is no guarantee that they either heard or understood it. Parents may expect to have this question asked, so should be ready with an answer.

J O E : What is sexual intercourse?

F A T H E R : It means the same thing as mating. Sometimes it is called the sex act. Sexual intercourse is when the sperm cells are put in the vagina so they can meet the ovum, or egg.

J O E : Yeah, I know that. What I want to know is how the sperm cells get into the vagina.

F A T H E R : Sexual intercourse is a very private and a very special way for married people to show they love each other. Married couples show their love for each other in many ways. I show my love for my wife and children by earning money so they will be able to buy the things they need. Mother shows her love by working for us at home. Sometimes a husband and wife show love for each other by kissing and hugging. The man has sperm cells and the woman has egg cells so they can have children that grow from the cells of their own bodies. Their bodies are made in such a way that man can put the sperms into the woman's body. When a husband and wife are lying close together and loving each other, the husband's penis can fit into the wife's vagina. At this time, semen and sperm leave the testicles, go through the penis, and enter the vagina. When semen and sperm go through the penis, no urine can pass through. If an egg cell happens to be in the wife's tube, it will be fertilized by a sperm and a new life will begin.

JOE: Is that how I started?

FATHER: Yes, you and Amy are both alive because you began while Mother and I were showing our love for each other. We say you are our most precious possession, because you came from our love and our bodies.

JOE: Do people have to be married to make it work?

FATHER: What do you think?

JOE: Well, I sort of think a grown man and a grown lady could do it, even if they aren't married.

FATHER: You're right about that, Joe. Do you think those people would have the same thoughts and love during sexual intercourse as a husband and wife?

JOE: No—If they did, wouldn't they want to get married? Do people ever do it?

FATHER: Yes, some people do, Joe. Young men and women often find each other very attractive, and they want to get well acquainted. You have heard that young people have dates. Well, they do this because they like to be together and want to know each other better. Before I met your mother, I found several pretty young women attractive and exciting to know, but I never wanted to make them my lifetime partner, my wife. When I met your mother, we had dates, and learned about each other. Then one day Mother and I discovered we loved each other very much. We both knew that we wanted to be married and live together and love each other for the rest of our lives. If I had

had sexual intercourse with the other young ladies I liked before I met Mother, would that have been good?

JOE: I think that would have been awful. I'll bet Mom would have been awful mad about it! I'll bet she wouldn't have married you!

FATHER: Yes, Joe, you are a very wise young man. Mother and I feel that sexual intercourse is only for husband and wife.

Timetables

Children want to know when and how they will change.

GIRL: What's the first thing that happens when I start to grow up to be a woman?

MOTHER: Well, let's see, I guess the first thing that happens is that you start to grow taller faster than usual, and you also gain some weight.

GIRL: You mean I'll get fat?

MOTHER: Oh no, not fat. You'll just gain weight a little faster, mostly because you're growing taller. Your shape changes a little, too. Usually the hips get a little larger.

GIRL: I've already started to grow taller. I was weighed at school, and I grew two inches this last year. What happens next?

MOTHER: Well, next you will start to grow breasts.

GIRL: Gosh, Mom, I've already started that. See? I think I should have a bra.

MOTHER: Not yet. You're just beginning to show the first signs of growth.

GIRL: Well, Mary has a bra. She said they are called training bras. Don't you think I should have a training bra?

MOTHER: Not yet, honey, but soon you will be ready for one.

GIRL: What happens next?

MOTHER: Remember, all this happens very slowly. It will take several years. The next thing you will notice is that a few hairs will grow in your armpits, and later some will grow on your lower abdomen.

GIRL: Why?

MOTHER: I really don't know why it grows there. Most women shave away the hair under their arms.

GIRL: I sure will. I think hair under the arms is creepy. What happens next?

MOTHER: Let's see. I guess the next thing is that your breasts will get larger, and you will menstruate.

GIRL: How old will I be then?

MOTHER: It's hard to tell. Sometimes girls menstruate at ten, and some don't start until they're sixteen or so. We are all different in many ways, and our growth patterns are different, also.

Boys, too, are curious about what they can expect during the years when they are growing into manhood.

BOY: Why do people say that boys mature slower than girls?

MOTHER: It means that their growth pattern is different from girls'. Most men grow taller than women, but they start their fast growing later than girls. Girls are usually as tall as they will get by the time they're seventeen or eighteen years old, while boys often keep right on growing until they're about twenty-one.

BOY: Do you ever wonder why boys grow slower?

MOTHER: When I was your age, I used to wonder about it. I think it's because boys' bones grow heavier before they start growing tall. Most men are taller and weigh more than women, and they need strong bones.

BOY: When will I start growing taller?

MOTHER: That's hard to tell. Most likely when you're twelve years old, or maybe older.

BOY: When will I get a man's voice?

MOTHER: You have a good deal of growing to do before that happens. About the time you're spurting up in size, you'll start to grow some hair under your arms and on the lower part of your abdomen. Your penis and sex organs will grow larger as you grow taller. About then your voice will gradually change.

BOY: We all laugh at Dave. When he talks, funny things happen. Sometimes when he starts to talk he squeaks, and then suddenly he sounds like himself. Once his voice sounded like his Dad's, and he said, "Hey, did that come out of me?" Boy, how we laughed.

MOTHER: Someday you'll be able to laugh at yourself, too.

BOY: When will I have to shave? Can I have an electric razor like Dad?

MOTHER: Someday you'll need a razor. Many boys start to shave in high school, and some don't need to until they're in college.

BOY: I hope I can shave when I'm in high school. I think it's fun to shave.

MOTHER: When you need to shave every morning, you'll wish the hair didn't grow on your face!

BOY: Hey, maybe I'll grow a beard!

MOTHER: Good grief—!

If sex education is not available in school, parents must assume full responsibility for their child's sex knowledge. It is recommended that such parents may also find helpful suggestions in the following chapter, which is intended primarily for teachers.

Chapter Twelve

The Preadolescent
at School

Behavior at school

Ten-year-old children are eager to have a teacher they like. Most of them respect her and accept her word as law. Above all, they want the teacher to treat all children fairly. They place great emphasis upon whether a teacher creates a friendly atmosphere in the classroom. Tens seem to learn best by listening, seeing, and talking things over. This is a receptive age for films, transparencies, educational TV, and microscopes.

Tens are aware of the teacher's clothes and hair and general physical appearance. Girls often comment to the teacher about her hair style or dress. They are still young enough to take the teacher's hand affectionately and even give her a quick kiss. If given the choice, the boys will all sit together in one part of the classroom and the girls in another part. Some girls are very aware of the boys and giggle when near them. The majority of boys pay little attention to girls. Boys are, however, interested in having boys treated as fairly as girls.

A teacher and her fifth-grade class were looking forward to a three-day outdoor educational workshop to be held at a camp. The workshop was sponsored by the school district for all fifth-grade children. A committee at the administration office made arrangements for sleeping quarters for the many children. All the girls in this particular classroom were to sleep in one cabin, while the boys were scheduled for another. The woman teacher was to be in charge of the girls' cabin while the male gym teacher was assigned to oversee the boys' cabin.

The teacher was reading the schedule for the three days, which she had just received from the planning committee, to the children. Excitement soared high, and the children clapped their hands and made happy noises whenever a particular scheduled event sounded especially interesting. At the end of the announcement, the teacher told the girls the name of the cabin they were scheduled for, and the boys the name of theirs.

TEACHER: *And Mr. Jones and I will be your cabin leaders.*
ALAN: *Whose cabin will you be in?*
TEACHER: *I'm scheduled to be in the girls' cabin.*
ALAN: *That's a gyp! The girls always get all the breaks. Why can't you be our cabin leader?*

All the boys complained bitterly that their regular teacher would be with the girls at night. Not one showed any awareness of why women teachers were assigned to girls' cabins and men teachers to the boys'.

Eleven-year-old children display less affection for their teacher, but sometimes get a crush on her, nevertheless. They like to stand around her and talk. Children this age want a teacher who expects them to work and who can keep order in the room. They resent being treated like babies, and complain bitterly if they feel this is the case. They expect the teacher to treat them fairly and to be patient, understanding, interesting, and above all never to "yell at them."

Twelve-year-old children are less dependent on their teacher. They like her if they feel she is a good teacher, but they rarely stand around and talk to her as they did at an earlier age. If the teacher is inexperienced or not too strong on discipline, twelves can make her life miserable. These children are becoming more independent in their schoolwork, books often take on a new and stronger appeal, and they display more enthusiasm for their classwork. Twelve-year-old children appear to feel they are traveling on steadier ground.

Twelve is more involved with his peers and likes being with a group. He feels secure and safe when he is one of the blending many. Girls especially seem always to be part of a cluster of girls, and often have boys as their topic of conversation.

Preadolescent needs

Helping children learn about growing up should be done before they are emotionally involved in the process themselves. When they know what to expect and why bodily changes are taking place, adolescence should have fewer uncertainties and concerns for them. Preparing a girl for menstruation after she has started to menstruate is an all-too-common occurrence.

The fifth grade seems to be a good time to place special emphasis upon teaching about reproduction and the series of changes that take place while growing from child to adult, for ten-year-old children are nearing the adolescent years. Tens regard and study the reproductive system in the same light and manner as the circulatory system. The majority of these children have not entered the transitional years and still have not identified themselves with adolescents, so they feel this study is about their nebulous future.

The following suggested unit may be presented in its entirety to fifth- or beginning sixth-grade children, or given in smaller segments during the fifth and sixth grades. The important objective is to be sure all children have had the opportunity to learn about puberty and reproduction.

Body systems

In the elementary school, sex education should not be set apart from other learning, as though it had no connection with other subjects presented in the classroom. One natural way to present it is to learn about the reproductive system along with the other body systems. Many teachers report that their children find the digestive system their "hang-up." This is the topic that makes them giggle and cast sidelong glances of embarrassment at their friends. The reproductive system does not cause nearly as great a reaction.

When starting the study of the body systems, which can be made fascinating for children, it is good to prepare them for it. The teacher may say, "We're going to start an interesting project. We will learn about us: what is inside of us, how we began life, how we stay alive, how we think and move, how we're nourished, and why each one of us is a unique individual.

"You haven't learned very much about how you are made on the inside, because you haven't been old enough up till now. It takes mature people to understand and to be scientifically interested in how our body systems work for us.

"We are going to use words which we normally don't use in our everyday conversations. They are words which we feel are private words. We will say such things as bowel movement and urinate. We must use these words if we want to understand about the digestive system. Young children often laugh and get silly when they hear or say any words connected with elimination. They can't learn about the body systems, for they get silly. I feel you are mature enough to enter into this study. If, however, any one of you feels insecure about yourself, you may tell me. I can arrange for you to work somewhere else during this time."

Naturally, no child will admit to being too immature. The first few times the teacher uses the words bowel movement or urine, all faces are tense and the eyes are unmoving. After becoming involved in the subject and hearing the words several times, the children will use them without hesitation. Soon all will be relaxed and deeply engrossed in learning.

The digestive system unit can be made more meaningful to children through the use of a torso model that has life-size organs of the body. The children can remove each organ to examine it and then replace it in its proper place. Films, books, transparencies, charts, and pictures all aid in understanding and visualizing the various organs that work together and are capable of taking food we eat and extracting nourishment for the many cells of our body.

By the end of this study, children will have gained a new feeling of wonder and appreciation for their bodies. Following the unit on the digestive system, the reproductive system seems to fit well into the complete systems study.

Cells and body growth

Having just learned how cells are nourished, the children can now discover how cells are important to reproduction.

TEACHER: *We learned that the nourishment that is taken by the digestive system from the food we eat is carried to the cells by the blood. What does this nourishment do for the cells?*
CHILD: *It feeds them so they can grow and be healthy.*

TEACHER: Right! And what do the cells often do when they grow large?

CHILD: I know! They divide, and then there are two cells.

TEACHER: You learned a great deal about cells last year. Do you remember why cells divide in our bodies?

CHILD: They divide to make more cells. More cells make more tissue, and that's how we all grow.

TEACHER: Yes, that is how you can grow taller. Do my cells divide?

CHILD: Sure.

TEACHER: Why? I'm not growing any taller.

CHILD: If you grew fatter, you would need more cells. Sometimes cells get worn out, and then you need new cells to take their place.

TEACHER: Are there any other ways to grow, besides taller or fatter?

CHILD: Skinnier?

TEACHER: I was thinking of maturing. It's true that most people grow taller when they mature, but other things happen also. Let's think about some of the changes we see when children start to mature.

GIRL: Girls begin to look different. They get a different shape, sorta.

TEACHER: Yes, girls do get a different shape. One thing that happens is that their pelvic bones grow larger. This makes a girl's hips larger. The bones are getting ready for the time when girls get married and become mothers. The pelvic bones will act like a cradle for the baby as it grows in the mother's uterus. As girls mature, breasts begin to grow. This, too, is part of growing up to be an adult. When women become mothers and give birth to a baby, milk will develop in their breasts for the baby. By the time a young lady has matured, we say she looks very feminine. It is the rounded hips, the narrow waist, and the bosom that gives her a feminine shape. When boys and girls are little, their shapes are similar.

BOY: Boys get different shapes, too. At least, I think men look different than little kids.

TEACHER: I agree. Can you tell us something that makes a man look different from a small boy?

C H I L D : *He's bigger.*

T E A C H E R : *Yes, but what else?*

C H I L D : *He grows hair on his face.*

T E A C H E R : *That's one change, but that doesn't affect his shape. Think about his shape, compared to a small boy's figure.*

C H I L D : *I know, it's his shoulders. They're bigger.*

T E A C H E R : *Right. A man's shoulders grow broader and bigger, and that makes his waist and hips look narrower. Why do you suppose his shoulders grow larger? A woman's shoulders usually don't get as large as a man's.*

C H I L D : *A man is strong and can do stronger work than a lady. His big shoulders and muscles make him strong.*

T E A C H E R : *Many years ago, before we could buy food and clothes and houses, did a man need tremendous strength?*

C H I L D : *Gosh, yes! The cave man had to kill animals with rocks and with his bare hands for food and clothes. He had to be able to move big rocks, and stuff like that.*

A N O T H E R C H I L D : *In pioneer days, it was almost as bad, except he had better tools. The pioneer had to catch and grow all his food, and he had to chop down trees and build his own house.*

T E A C H E R : *Those big, strong shoulders and arms were absolutely necessary to stay alive in the days you told about. What about today?*

C H I L D : *Some men work hard, like furniture movers and farmers and men who build houses and apartments. But my Dad doesn't work hard. He says he sits all day at his desk.*

A N O T H E R C H I L D : *My dad doesn't need to be strong at work, but he likes to use his muscles at home. He mows the lawn and carries heavy stuff for Mom. He even does exercises with dumbbells. Boy, you should see his muscles! He's awfully strong!*

Pictures showing silhouettes of babies, children, adolescents, and adults are intriguing for ten-year-olds to study. They often decide they look more like the child's silhouette, but some are sure they are beginning to resemble the adolescent.

Children enjoy making charts, books, transparencies, and other visuals to tell about the many things they study. In a classroom all these different projects can be going on at the same time. Several children may decide to make a book about growing up, particularly if the teacher suggests they could make a bound, hard-cover book (which she will guide them in making). Suggesting that this could be presented to the school library, so that all the children in the school can enjoy it, will raise the standard of the finished book immediately. Written stories and illustrations, added to the book as the study progresses, will add up to a good overview of the unit.

Several children can make charts their project. Hanging well-made charts in the classroom sparks up any unit of study for the children. Making transparencies to use on the overhead projector, or pictures for the opaque projector, always brings great satisfaction to the young artists, and they find it easier to talk on a subject when they are using a projector as an aid. Pictures of babies, children, and adults taken from magazines will stimulate children's ideas for their pictures, diagrams, and charts.

As work begins on the projects, the teacher may suggest, "These charts and transparencies you are making are so interesting and well done that an idea just flashed through my mind."

"What is it?" will immediately be asked by the curious children.

"Why don't we plan to invite your parents to come to school when we finish learning about growing up? We can tell them about the things we are studying and show them our pictures and books and everything we make." Nothing seems to stimulate learning and creative ideas and effort more than the promise of sharing it all with others.

TEACHER: We have been learning about how people grow taller and change their shapes as they mature, because cells divide and make new cells. We learned that cells cluster together to make tissue. Are the cells and tissue all alike? Do all the cells make us taller or wider?

CHILD: Some cells make the heart tissue and some make the skin and some the muscles and some the bones. I remember last year we learned that each cell makes only its own kind.

TEACHER: You said there are many different kinds of cells, and this is true. You also said that each kind of cell makes only its own kind. How does that happen?

CHILD: Well, there's a nucleus in each cell which tells the cell what it should be. When a cell divides, the nucleus divides too, and so each cell gets to be told the same thing.

TEACHER: Yes, the nucleus determines what the cell's function is. What would happen if a cell divided and somehow the nucleus did not divide, and the new daughter cell did not have a nucleus?

CHILD: The cell without a nucleus would just die. It can't make a new cell without a nucleus, it can't even do its job without a nucleus.

TEACHER: The nucleus is most important. Do you remember what is in the nucleus? It is very important to all of us.

CHILD: I do! Chromosomes.

TEACHER: Does anyone remember how many chromosomes are in each human cell nucleus? (Silence.) Well, I'll tell you. Scientists believe there are forty-six chromosomes. Something even smaller is on each chromosome. Does anyone remember what it is?

CHORUS: It's genes!

CHILD: Genes are what make us inherit things from our parents and ancestors.

TEACHER: What kind of things?

CHILD: Oh, like the color of our eyes or the shape of our nose, or how big or little we are when we grow up.

TEACHER: Yes, that's right. Each cell in our body has forty-six chromosomes and many genes. Half of these chromosomes and genes you inherited from your father and his two parents, and his four grandparents, and eight great-grandparents, and on back. The other half you inherited from your mother and her two parents, and four grandparents, and on back. Did you inherit all forty-six chromosomes from your mother and all forty-six from your father?

CHILD: We couldn't! Half came from Mother, half from Father. Each of our cells has forty-six chromosomes, so we got twenty-three chromosomes from Mother and her ancestors, and twenty-three from Father and his ancestors.

TEACHER: Good thinking! We don't know which of the twenty-three you inherited from your mother and which twenty-three from your father. The combination makes you look different from your father and different from your mother, yet some parts of you resemble each one. Do you realize that the combination of chromosomes and genes you inherited makes you look different from anyone else on earth?

We have learned a great deal about how children's bodies change on the outside as they mature into young adults, but what happens inside of the body during these changing years?

CHILD: Our organs grow bigger?

TEACHER: True, the organs do grow as the body grows, but something very special becomes mature. The sex organs mature. Right below the brain is a small gland, about the size of a grape, called the pituitary gland. Sometimes it is called a growth clock. When a child reaches a certain age, this growth clock releases chemical messengers—hormones —that awaken the reproductive glands. The reproductive glands then give off hormones that influence growth. As we learned, a girl's shape changes to prepare her for being a mother when she is grown, and a boy's shape changes to make him the father and strong protector.

Inside of a girl's body, the reproductive organs begin to mature.

At this point, a simple diagram may be drawn on the board by the teacher, showing the ovaries, Fallopian tubes, uterus, and vagina. On a later occasion an overhead projector transparency of the reproductive system may be used, but initially children enjoy the piece-by-piece drawing done by the teacher. Draw the two small, almond-shaped ovaries first, then ask the children, "Do you know what these two small things I have drawn represent?" Undoubtedly no child will know.

TEACHER: These are ovaries. Does anyone remember what ova are?

CHILD: I do, ova means eggs.

TEACHER: Right. Ova is the Latin word for eggs. Then what do you think ovary means?

CHILD: Many eggs?

TEACHER: You're close, but that's not quite correct.

CHILD: Is it something that eggs are in?

TEACHER: Yes, that's right. When a baby girl is born, she has thousands of egg cells in the ovaries. Many, many more than she can ever use. When the pituitary gland sends out hormones that awaken the ovaries, some egg cells begin to grow. One at a time the eggs ripen or mature. About once each month an egg will ripen and enter a Fallopian tube. Usually an ovum, or egg, is released from one ovary. The next month an ovum is released from the other ovary. (At this point the teacher may sketch in the Fallopian tubes.) These are tubes, called the Fallopian tubes. There is one for each ovary. These tubes lead to a small pear-shaped organ called the uterus. (Sketch in the uterus.) You know what the uterus is for, don't you?

CHILD: Yes. It's the special place where babies grow.

TEACHER: The uterus is about the size and shape of a pear, or your fist. Is that big enough for a baby to grow in?

CHILD: It will be big enough, because the uterus stretches as the baby grows.

TEACHER: I see that you children know a great deal about the reproductive system. (Sketch in the vagina.) This is often called the birth canal, because the baby goes through it when it is being born. It has another name. Does anyone know that name?

CHILD: Yes, the vagina.

TEACHER: Good. Let's go back and name all the parts

again. I'll write the names to label each part. (Keep the sketch of the female reproductive organ on the blackboard, as the male organ is sketched and discussed.)

The male reproductive organs begin to mature when a boy matures into a man. The male reproductive glands are called testicles, or testes. They are small and are in a sac of skin called the scrotum, which hangs between the legs of the male. The pituitary gland in a boy also sends out hormones at the proper time, which awaken his sex glands, the testes. Sperm cells begin to develop by the million in the testes. There are times when sperm, in a whitish fluid called semen, are released from the testes. They are released through the penis. Sperm and semen never go through the penis at the same time that urine is discharged.

This is often enough for one day's lesson. By breaking the story of reproduction into smaller segments, it offers the opportunity each day to quickly review the material presented previously.

Fertilization of ova

Telling children the story of how an ovum is fertilized and starts new life should be done in simple, understandable terms. Questions they ask should be answered in the same manner. The conversations in this book are planned to give the reader a feeling or suggestion of how to talk to children about sex and reproduction, and are not intended to be used verbatim. Each teacher has her own way of speaking to her children and, as all teachers know, each group and its particular needs differ.

Following a review of the male and female reproductive organs, the story of fertilization and menstruation may be told in this way.

TEACHER: The story of how new life begins is a very interesting one. As you know, when a girl matures one ovum, or egg, each month matures or ripens. This ovum leaves the ovary and enters a Fallopian tube. Fine waving hairs inside of the Fallopian tube gently push the ovum through to the uterus. It takes five or six days to travel through the tube, which is roughly four inches long. (Draw a round ovum in a tube.)

While this is happening to the ovum, the uterus is getting ready for it. Do you know how it gets ready?

CHILD: I heard that the lining of the uterus gets extra blood.

TEACHER: Yes, it does. The lining of the uterus thickens and becomes soft and spongy, and an extra supply of blood is also provided in the lining. The uterus has prepared for the fertilized ovum. If the ovum is fertilized and starts a new life, the uterus is waiting and ready to help that new life grow.

If the egg is not fertilized, it will soon die and disintegrate. When this happens, the soft lining and extra blood are not needed, for there is no new life to help and nourish. So the unneeded lining of the uterus, with the extra supply of blood, comes off and is slowly discharged through the vagina. (Sketch picture of extra lining and blood leaving uterus.) This is called menstruation. This happens each month when an ovum leaves an ovary and is not fertilized.

(Draw a quick sketch of a woman's sex organs again.) Now we will find out how an ovum is fertilized, and how the uterus helps the new life. I will draw an ovum in a tube again, but this time it won't disintegrate. What must happen to the ovum to start a baby?

CHILD: It has to be fertilized.

TEACHER: What will fertilize it?

CHILD: A sperm cell from the male.

TEACHER: Yes, a male sperm. The sperm and semen enter the woman's body through the vagina. The sperm are many, many times smaller than the ovum. They have long hairlike tails which help them move through the semen up the walls of the vagina, and then up through the uterus and into the two tubes. Many sperm are not strong enough to make that long journey, and only the strongest sperm will reach the ovum. One strong sperm will enter, or join with the ovum, and all the other sperm will die. The minute the sperm unites with the ovum, new life begins. Can anyone tell us why?

CHILD: Because it takes a male and a female to start a new life.

TEACHER: That is correct, but why does it take a male and a female?

CHILD: Because the egg cell isn't complete unless an ovum and sperm unite.

TEACHER: Correct, but what makes it complete? It is a very amazing story of how the cell becomes complete. The ovum is a tiny egg, smaller than this dot I made on the blackboard, but it has a yolk and it has a nucleus. But the nucleus is not complete. It has only twenty-three chromosomes, and all cells in a human being have how many chromosomes?

CHILD: Forty-six.

TEACHER: Right, forty-six. So the ovum nucleus has only half enough chromosomes. The sperm cell, too, has a nucleus, but it also has only twenty-three chromosomes.

CHILD: I get it! When the ovum and sperm unite, the cells become one complete cell with forty-six chromosomes. Then the cell can grow and divide.

TEACHER: Very good. That is correct. The sperm and ovum usually unite in the Fallopian tube. The new complete cell soon divides into two cells and the nucleus and chromosomes and genes also divide so that each cell will be complete. Then the two cells divide again and there are four cells, and the four cells divide and there are eight, and so on. These dividing cells stay clustered together like this. (Draw sketch of dividing cells.)

By the time it reaches the uterus, it is a little cluster of many cells. What has happened to the uterus while the cells have been dividing and multiplying in the tube?

CHILD: The uterus lining got thicker and softer, like a sponge, and it has more blood than it usually does.

TEACHER: And the ball of cells uses the lining as a soft nest. The blood helps to nourish the cells, which continue to divide and grow. Before long, the cells change themselves into three layers; one layer makes the brains, spinal cord, nerves, and skin; another layer will produce the stomach, intestines, liver, and pancreas; the third layer will make the skeleton, heart, blood vessels, muscles, and so on, until a new human being has been produced.

A placenta and umbilical cord will also grow. For the first two months of his life, the baby will be called an embryo. When he begins to look like a human being he is called a fetus.

CHILD: What is the placenta and umbilical cord?

TEACHER: The placenta is a very special organ that forms on the inner wall of the uterus. It is made largely of blood vessels. Some of the blood vessels are the baby's and some are the mother's. One end of the umbilical cord is attached to the placenta and the other end is attached to the baby. A membrane sac, called an amnion, grows around the baby. In the sac is a fluid called amniotic fluid, in which the baby floats. This sac and fluid keep the delicate new life safe. Does anyone know what the umbilical cord does for the baby?

CHILD: Food goes through the tube to the baby.

TEACHER: Where does the cord get the food, or nourishment?

CHILD: From the placenta.

TEACHER: Where does the placenta get food?

CHILD: It produces food. It is sort of like a manufacturing company.

TEACHER: That's a pretty good description. The placenta doesn't really make food and oxygen, it transports it. The mother's blood brings oxygen and nourishment to the placenta. You all remember, when we were studying the digestive system we learned how the blood stream picks up nourishment that goes through the walls of the intestines. The blood also picks up oxygen when it reaches the lungs. This is how the mother's blood is able to bring nourishment and oxygen to the placenta.

The placenta transfers oxygen and nourishment to the baby's blood in the umbilical cord. The baby's blood then takes the nourishment and oxygen to the developing baby. After two months the baby begins to look like a very small person with a large head, small body, and tiny arms and legs. When this happens, it is no longer called an embryo, but a fetus.

The fetus

Children should always be given an opportunity to ask questions. Some of their questions will be about the very things the teacher felt she had explained so well. But children miss many parts of an explanation while their minds dwell on one specific bit of information. Some questions will be only one child's particular concern, but it too must be answered.

CHILD: How does the baby eat?

TEACHER: Good question. Who can answer it?

CHILD: I know, the mother's blood brings nourishment and oxygen to the placenta. The placenta transfers it to the baby through the umbilical cord. The fetus doesn't eat meat and potatoes with its mouth.

TEACHER: Does that answer your question? Any more questions?

CHILD: I don't understand how the father puts the sperms into the mother's vagina.

TEACHER: A husband and wife often show how much they love each other. They like to be close and hug and kiss each other. They are very loving to one another in many ways. They may want a baby to add to their love. For a baby to grow, we know that a sperm and ovum must unite. This can only happen during mating, or sexual intercourse. At this time the male sex organ releases semen and sperm through the husband's penis, which he places in his wife's vagina. This is how sperm get into the vagina. Sometimes when a husband and wife have sexual intercourse, no baby starts to grow, for there may not be an ovum in the tube. Who remembers how often an ovum is released from the ovary?

CHILD: I know, once every month.

TEACHER: Correct. You are all learning and remembering so well.

CHILD: You said the baby floats in a fluid. How come the baby doesn't drown?

TEACHER: To drown, a person must have his supply of

oxygen cut off. You know that the fetus gets any oxygen he needs from the blood. The baby does suck in and swallow some fluid, but he doesn't use his nose and mouth to breathe inside the sac.

CHILD: How does the baby go to the toilet inside the uterus?

TEACHER: The fetus doesn't eat food as you and I do. When food is eaten, bowel movements are necessary to carry off wastes. The fetus receives nourishment through the blood. Any waste material that comes from the growing fetus is removed through the blood vessel in the umbilical cord to the placenta. Here waste is picked up and removed by the mother's blood stream.

Most fifth-graders have learned quite a good deal about the fetus and his environment from home or previous classroom experiences. However, a quick review and answering of questions is good for those who feel they already know, and it is very necessary for any children who have not received their information from parents or teachers.

TEACHER: Why is the baby growing in a sac of fluid?

CHILD: If the mother falls, the baby won't be hurt. The water protects it.

TEACHER: Yes, the fluid sac acts as a shock absorber. The fluid also helps the baby to be comfortable. When the fetus is small, it can move and float and dive around in the fluid. This is good exercise for the fetus. It can also move its arms and legs easily in the fluid.

CHILD: I heard that the fluid always stays the same temperature, whether the mother is out walking in zero weather or when it's ninety degrees.

TEACHER: Even temperature is most important for the fetus. I'm glad you mentioned the temperature. Isn't it amazing that our built-in thermostats can keep our temperature constant?

CHILD: The umbilical cord looks awful long. Couldn't the baby get all wound up in it?

TEACHER: Looking at a picture makes one think that

the umbilical cord would cause problems; but it cannot possibly get knotted or wound tightly around the fetus, for the cord is too stiff and slippery.

CHILD: Does the baby cry before it's born? Does the mother ever hear her baby cry?

TEACHER: The baby may cry, but you wouldn't hear it. Do you know why?

CHILD: The sac doesn't let the noise get through?

TEACHER: No, the sac cannot do that. For you to hear my voice, what must happen?

CHILD: I know, sound waves travel through the air from your mouth to my ears.

TEACHER: Right. Inside the sac, the baby is floating in a liquid. There is not enough air to produce sound waves. No air from the baby's lungs passes over the vocal cords.

CHILD: Why are the babies upside down in the uterus?

TEACHER: They aren't always upside down; only when they get large. The last few weeks before birth, the fetus grows rapidly and nearly fills up all the space in the uterus. He finds that he is most comfortable head down because of the shape of the uterus.

CHILD: When I stand on my head a long time, the blood rushes to my head and I feel funny. Doesn't the baby feel funny?

TEACHER: You have seen on TV how astronauts float around in outer space because there is no gravity. They don't feel any different upside down from right side up. The baby, too, lacks the pull of gravity in its little space ship, which is the sac in the uterus.

CHILD: How long does it take for a baby to grow in the uterus?

TEACHER: Nine months. Sometimes a baby is born before that time. Such a baby usually is kept in an incubator and given special care. Babies born before the full term of nine months are called premature babies.

CHILD: Why is a baby born before he is ready?

TEACHER: I really don't know. I do know that there are a variety of causes. A doctor is the one qualified to answer your question.

The baby is born

Children are interested in hearing about the birth of a baby. They want to know how and where he comes out and whether it hurts the baby and the mother.

TEACHER: When the fetus has been growing for nine months, he is getting too large to be comfortable in the uterus. He is squeezed tightly, for the uterus can stretch no further. As he tries to move his arms and legs, his head pushes against the cervix, which is the opening that leads to the vagina. The muscles of the uterus start to contract and tighten and push downward on the baby. This causes the baby's head to push harder and harder against the opening. Gradually the muscle contractions—called labor pains—push the baby through the vagina—or birth canal —and out into the world.

CHILD: Does it hurt the mother when the baby is born?

TEACHER: Yes, there are usually some sharp pains, but mothers accept those pains gladly to have a baby. Doctors can give mothers some pain-killing medicines which make the birth less painful.

CHILD: Does it hurt the baby to be pushed out?

TEACHER: I'm sure it must hurt the baby a little. Also, leaving the warm, comfortable uterus and suddenly being in a brightly lighted room, with air all around him instead of fluid, is quite a shock to the baby. He often sucks in a big gulp of something he has never experienced before— who knows what that is?

CHILDREN: Air!

TEACHER: Right! His first breath of air. It shocks him so that he usually starts to cry lustily. Sometimes he doesn't start to breathe by himself. Do you know what the doctor does then?

CHILD: He holds him upside down by his legs, and gives him a spank.

TEACHER: Yes, he gives the baby a sharp spank. Well, this is just too much for the baby to accept. First he leaves his comfortable nest, then he is squeezed and pushed, then bright lights shine all around, and for the first time he is touched by hands. As if that isn't enough to make him angry, he gets a spanking. He wails out in protest, and suddenly he has taken a big breath of air. From now on he must do his own breathing.

CHILD: Is the umbilical cord still attached to the baby?

TEACHER: Yes, but the baby won't need it now that he is born, so the doctor cuts it off and puts a little bandage on the baby where it was cut. That is why each one of you has a navel. It's a little scar showing where you were once attached to your umbilical cord. The placenta is also pushed out of the uterus, for the baby will not need it any longer.

CHILD: Won't the next baby need it?

TEACHER: No, because each baby has his own placenta and his own umbilical cord.

CHILD: Does the baby come out of the place where the urine comes out?

TEACHER: No, the baby has a special opening through which he comes. A woman has three openings between her legs. The first small opening in front is used for urine. In the middle is the vagina opening, and the third opening in the back is called an anus, and it is used for bowel movements.

CHILD: Doesn't it hurt the baby when the umbilical cord is cut?

TEACHER: No, because there are no nerves in the cord.

CHILD: What happens to the fluid in the sac? Does it get born with the baby?

TEACHER: Sometime during the birth, the sac breaks from the pressure, and the fluid goes out. The fluid makes it a little easier for the baby to get through the vagina and the openings.

CHILD: How did pioneers have babies? There weren't any hospitals near, were there?

TEACHER: The pioneer mother had her baby in her own home. Someone in her family helped with the birth. Most babies were born safely. If a baby had trouble starting to breathe, the baby sometimes died. Today the hospitals have doctors who have studied many years about babies and how they are born. Their knowledge and modern equipment help babies live.

CHILD: I'm glad I'm living today and not in pioneer days. I wouldn't want my baby to die.

TEACHER: Most mothers are happy to be in a hospital when their baby is born. It's nice for them to be cared for by nurses for a day or two after the baby is born. They know their precious baby is being given the best of care in the nursery at the hospital.

Unwed mothers

In a classroom where children feel secure and know each question and thought they have is respected, some child will undoubtedly wonder and ask about the possibility of having a baby grow without being married. If the question is not asked, a teacher should approach the subject herself.

CHILD: If an eleven- or twelve-year-old girl starts to have eggs ripen, could she have a baby?

TEACHER: She is physically capable.

CHILD: But she wouldn't be married at eleven or twelve.

TEACHER: No, she wouldn't.

CHILD: Has it ever happened?

TEACHER: Yes, it has. I'm very glad you asked that question, for I would like to hear your opinions and ideas about a twelve-year-old girl being a mother.

Opinions, ideas, and suggestions usually follow quickly, after the shocking realization of this possibility.

"A twelve-year-old girl may be able to have a baby, but she couldn't be a real mother. Who wants a mother that's a kid!"

"I feel sorry for the baby!"

"Who would the father be?"

"There wouldn't be a father, 'cause they wouldn't be married."

"The girl wouldn't get the baby all alone. There has to be a father."

"After all, her ovum is only half a cell. It takes a father sperm to make the cell grow a baby."

"Yeah, maybe there wasn't a father, but some kid must have thought he was a father. Boy, he was dumb!"

"Yeah, well the girl was dumb, too!"

"I sure wouldn't want a baby when I'm in junior high!"

"How can kids be so stupid?"

"Maybe they didn't know. Maybe their mothers and fathers didn't tell them."

"Well, they could have learned in school, if they'd listened."

TEACHER: *Not all schools teach about reproduction.*
CHILD: *How come?*
TEACHER: *Some people feel that reproduction should be taught only at home.*

The responses to this statement will also be varied.

"My Mom doesn't teach me about it."

"Maybe that girl's mom didn't teach her. I think the teacher should have told her."

"Me, too!"

"What do they do with the baby? They aren't married!"

"They can get married."

"How can a kid father earn enough money to take care of a wife and a baby?"

"Maybe they could live with their mother and father."

"That sounds silly."

"I feel sorry for the baby. How can it have a home?"

"Maybe someone will adopt the baby."

"Yeah, that would be better."

"There are lots of married people who don't have

babies, and they want babies something awful. I bet they would be glad to have that baby."

"That would be nice for the baby. Every baby should have good parents. Who would want kids for parents!"

"Wouldn't that girl feel bad about not having her baby?"

"Maybe she would feel bad, but a baby doesn't want a kid for a mother."

"Why would two kids have sexual intercourse, anyway?"

TEACHER: *That's a good question. Why do you suppose they would do such a thing?*

"Maybe the guy thought he was tough and a big shot."

"Kids shouldn't do such things to each other."

"When kids do it, it sounds dirty."

"Yeah, it's not only dirty, but dumb, too."

These are typical responses a teacher may expect. Usually, some child will say he or she has heard about unwed mothers or knows one personally. The children's frank discussion is helping them to understand the full significance of sexual intercourse outside of wedlock. The discussion certainly helps them in gaining attitudes of responsibility and respect for themselves and others.

If the teacher had found the question too embarrassing for her to handle and had ignored it, she would have denied the children the opportunity to learn and build attitudes and understanding of what is good and what is bad.

Boy or girl?

Children are always curious about what sex a new baby will be. Those who have had a recent birth occur in their family will tell how anxious everyone was to know whether the new arrival was a boy or a girl.

Before long the conversation will bring up the question of how baby boys happen and how baby girls happen, and whether parents have any way of deciding the sex of their baby.

TEACHER: *Parents don't know whether the baby is a girl or boy until it is born.*

CHILD: *Does the baby start right out growing to be a boy or girl? How does it know what to be?*

TEACHER: *Yes, the baby starts right out being a boy baby or girl baby, the minute the sperm and ovum unite. We have talked a good deal about chromosomes. Each cell in a human being's body has two sex chromosomes. The female has two X chromosomes in each cell of her body. The male has one X chromosome and one Y chromosome in each cell in his body. We learned that an ovum has only twenty-three chromosomes. Do you remember?*

CHILD: *I remember. It's sort of like half a cell. The sperm is like half a cell, too, because it only has twenty-three chromosomes, too.*

TEACHER: *Right. Since the two sex chromosomes in each female's body cells are X, what will the one sex chromosome be in her ovum?*

CHILDREN: An X chromosome.

TEACHER: *Correct. The male's two sex chromosomes in each of his body cells are not alike. Do you remember what they are?*

CHILD: *One is an X chromosome and one is a Y chromosome.*

TEACHER: *The sperm is like the ovum and has only half the regular chromosomes. So some sperm that are produced may have one Y chromosome and the other sperm may have the X chromosome. As we know, only one sperm will unite with the ovum. If that sperm happens to have an X chromosome, then the X one of the ovum and the X one of the sperm will make two X chromosomes in the united, complete cell.*

CHILD: *Now I get it! Females have two X chromosomes*

in each body cell, so the new cell that united will grow
a female baby.

TEACHER: That is exactly right. Now who can tell us
how a baby boy begins to grow? Goodness, almost all of
you have your hands up! John, you tell us.

JOHN: If the sperm cell that unites with the ovum
happens to have a Y chromosome, then the new complete
cell will have a Y chromosome and the ovum's X chromosome. Since all male body cells have an X and a Y chromosome, this new cell will grow to be a boy baby. (A sketch
of the X and Y chromosomes and cells on the blackboard
or overhead projector will add to the understanding of the
sex heredity.)

Multiple births

Any unusual occurrence always seems to fascinate the
preadolescent child, and so they are normally curious
about multiple births. Twins are usually asked about
first, for they are the most common of the multiple
births. Roughly one in every eighty pregnancies results
in twins. Triplets are much more unusual. They occur
only once in more than six thousand pregnancies.
Quadruplets occur roughly once in every five hundred
thousand, and quintuplets once in every forty million
or more pregnancies.

The ten- and eleven-year-old children are interested
in learning the difference between identical twins and
fraternal twins. They may be told that identical twins
are from one ovum and one sperm. When the two cells
unite and become one complete cell with forty-six chromosomes, the cell soon divides. Almost always the cells
cluster together and remain as one sphere of cells. In
the case of identical twins, the first division of the fertilized ovum breaks the ovum into two parts. Then
each part will develop in the same way as a regular
ovum through cell division. The two babies born will
be of the same sex and have an identical inheritance

from chromosomes and genes, because they both are the result of the same ovum and the same sperm. Identical twins closely resemble one another.

Fraternal twins are no more alike than any two siblings in a family. Fraternal twins develop from separate ova that have each been fertilized by a different sperm. Occasionally the ovaries release two ova at about the same time instead of one. If sperm are present, both eggs have the chance of being fertilized. Two girls, two boys, or a boy and a girl may result in this kind of multiple birth. Each has inherited a different combination of chromosomes and genes, since they developed from different ova and sperm.

Triplets, too, can be identical and result from one ovum and one sperm. When an egg divides and splits into two separate parts, one part of the split cells may also split again into two separate parts, resulting in identical triplets. If both parts split, identical quadruplets would result. Triplets can also be nonidentical, by growing from three separate ova.

In the same ways, quintuplets and other multiple births can occur. In one recorded set of quintuplets, two of the children were identical and came from one ovum, two other children were identical and grew from another ovum, while the fifth child grew from the third ovum.

Siamese twins invariably are brought into the discussion, because of their rarity and because they are joined. This occurs when an ovum splits into two parts, the way it does for identical twins; but in the case of Siamese twins the split is not quite complete.

Separating the sexes

The physical maturing of both sexes has been presented and discussed in the classroom. However, children may

have questions they prefer asking only in the presence
of their own sex. For this reason it seems to be a good
idea that the boys meet once separately with a male
teacher, principal, or doctor, or a combination of several. Girls can meet with the classroom teacher and a
school nurse or gym teacher. The girls may be better
served if all three are present.

The leader of each group could give a short review
on physical changes their sex can anticipate in the near
future. A carefully chosen film can serve the same purpose. With this as a springboard, questions will follow.
Boys may question the differences in growth and size.
They may have heard of seminal emissions and are
seeking an honest explanation. Some boys may be disturbed about masturbation (although they will never
hint that it is their problem) and wonder if the stories
they have been told are true.

The girls' film or review can be on menstruation.
There are many questions girls have about this. The
school nurse or teacher can show the girls a sanitary
pad (or napkin) and belt. Telling them what to do if
they should start to menstruate at school and are not
prepared will be eagerly listened to by the girls. How
to dispose of the pad when changing to a fresh one is
of equal concern to them. Learning that gym classes,
after-school play, and other exercise can continue during the menstruation period is necessary for them to
know. Reminding the girls that all women menstruate
puts less personal emphasis on it. Occasionally some
child will ask if grandmothers menstruate. Menopause,
which normally takes place around forty-five to fifty
years of age, can be explained to them. Keeping this
class as informal as possible encourages discussion.
When the class comes to an end, the girls usually cluster around the teachers, continuing to ask their endless
questions.

One question that will undoubtedly be asked, due to the widespread publicity it has received in newspapers and magazines, is "What is the pill? Will I use it?"

Out of respect for the different religious backgrounds of the children, a teacher must not express her opinion on whether she approves of the use of it or not. She may want to say, "The pill is given by a doctor to any married woman who wishes to regulate the size of her family." If further questions are asked, it may be best to advise the girls to discuss this with their parents, because parents often have differing views on the acceptance of the pill.

Teaching aids

Films and transparencies can be helpful to a teacher in telling the story of reproduction and learning about families and people. Children benefit more from these visual aids if a background of information has been given before viewing them.

There are many transparencies which will stimulate discussion, questions, and learning in a classroom. These visual aids do not take the place of teaching. For a teacher to show a film on reproduction and consider her contribution to the child's sex education as finished is doing more harm than good. Wholesome, respectful attitudes toward sex and human sexuality cannot be built under such circumstances.

All films and transparencies must be thoroughly reviewed by teachers and school authorities prior to classroom presentation. Teachers and school supervisors should choose films and transparencies appropriate for their particular children. Not all transparencies in a set need necessarily be shown. The teacher has the privilege of selecting those that will benefit her children.

Books that are selected to be put in the classroom

must also be thoughtfully screened as to their appropriateness for individual study.

Parent involvement

Parents should be invited to the school prior to starting the family living–sex education in the classroom. Stressing attendance at the meeting often aids in reaching more parents.

A review of the procedures and aims that the school has planned to use in helping children learn about families and people and sex, showing parents the films their children will see and encouraging their questions, gives parents the opportunity to understand the school's program and its interest in their child's total education. This type of meeting often helps parents learn how to talk to their own child about sex.

Teachers should be prepared to recommend to parents, upon their inquiring, books that parent and child can read and discuss together. Many parents are concerned about their own meager background in sex education and their inability or hesitation to talk to their own children about sex. The schools should provide or recommend books which will be helpful to these parents.

Sixth- and seventh-grade children

Sixth- and seventh-grade children are often concerned about the new feelings they have, the apprehensions and perplexities. Most of them want to talk about themselves and how they feel, discover why they are often at odds with adults, why marijuana is bad, why people take narcotics, why there are homosexuals, how a person gets venereal disease, and so on and on. The more mature twelve-year-olds concern themselves with problems of how to be popular, how to act on a date, and whether boys are expected to kiss girls when they are together. There are always a few children who have been influenced by older teen-agers and who wonder "how far" to go with the opposite sex. These children all want straight answers and the true facts, and they must have them. Many junior-high youngsters are exposed to narcotics by unscrupulous peddlers or by their peers. Some are approached by sex deviates. Their questions must be answered and the facts given to them.

Eleven's and twelve's eagerness to be one of the gang makes it difficult for him to go against the dictates of the group. He may easily become unhappily involved in affairs he knows are wrong, because of his desire to be popular. Schools must help these children and must reach each and every one before trouble overtakes them. They need to be made aware of and to understand the many temptations they will meet, what they can expect if they yield to them, and how to handle pressures intelligently.

Specially trained teachers should conduct regularly held classes starting at the sixth or seventh grade to help children maintain good mental health, reach for the best in their environment, and attain pleasure in their own sexuality.

Surely each child deserves the chance to reach upward toward happiness and a full life. The home, church, and school, working together, can guide each child toward his goal.

Glossary

Amnion (*AM-nee-on*). The sac containing the amniotic fluid and the growing baby.

Anus (*A-nus*). The opening of the rectum through which solid wastes of digestion pass.

Cervix (*SER-vix*). The neck of the uterus leading to the vagina.

Embryo (*EM-bree-oh*). In humans, the first stages of the developing baby until about the end of the second month of development.

Fallopian (*fa-LO-pee-an*) **tubes.** A pair of slender tubes for transporting ova from the ovaries to the uterus.

Fertilization (*FUR-tuh-luh-ZAY-shun*). The union of the male sperm and female ovum.

Fetus (*FEE-tus*). In humans, the developing baby from near the beginning of the third month until birth.

Homosexual (*hoh-mo-SEK-shoo-al*). One who satisfies his sexual desires with a member of his own sex.

Hormone (*HOR-mown*). A body chemical produced by a gland that is carried by the blood stream to stimulate the functioning of parts of the body.

Masturbation (mas-tur-BAY-shun). Sexual stimulation by manipulation of the genital organs.

Menstruation (men-stroo-AY-shun). The monthly flow of waste blood, secretions, and uterine lining from the uterus.

Navel (NAY-vel). A depression in the middle of the abdomen at the point where the umbilical cord was attached.

Ovary (OH-vuh-ree). An almond-shaped female reproductive organ in which ova develop and sex hormones are produced.

Ovum (OH-vum), plural ova (OH-vuh). A female egg cell.

Penis (PEE-nus). The male sex organ through which urine and semen pass out of the body.

Pituitary (pi-TYOO-uh-ter-ee). A small oval gland situated below the brain. It regulates growth and other maturing functions of the body.

Scrotum (SKROH-tum). The external sac of skin in which the testicles hang between the male's legs.

Seminal emissions (SEM-i-nal ee-MISH-uns). The passing of semen through the penis during sleep.

Sperm cell (spurm sel), plural sperm. A male sex cell. Its scientific name is spermatozoon.

Testis (TESS-tiss), plural testes (TESS-teez). Two glands contained in the human male which produce sperm cells.

Umbilical (um-BILL-i-cal) cord. The cord which connects the baby to the placenta within the uterus.

Urethra (*yoo-REE-thra*). A membranous tube through which urine passes from the bladder to the exterior. In a male, it also conveys semen.

Uterus (*YOO-ter-us*) or **womb** (*woom*). A hollow organ of the female reproductive system in which the fertilized ovum grows into a baby.

Vagina (*vuh-JY-nuh*). The passageway between the uterus and the outside of the body.

Vulva (*VUL-vuh*). The folds of skin and other structures which protect the opening of the vagina.

Bibliography

Books parents and teachers may find useful

Arnstein, Helene S. Your Growing Child and Sex. Indianapolis: Bobbs-Merrill Co., 1967

Bueltmann, A. J. Take the High Road. St. Louis: Concordia Publishing House, 1967.

Child Study Association of America. What To Tell Your Child about Sex. New York: Arco Publishing Co., 1961.

Ginott, Dr. Haim G. Between Parent and Child. New York: The Macmillan Company, 1965.

Kolb, Erwin J. A Parent's Guide to Christian Conversation about Sex. St. Louis: Concordia Publishing House, 1967.

Lerrigo, Marion O. and Cassidy, Michael. A Doctor Talks to 9-to-12-Year-Olds. Chicago: Budlong Press, 1967.

Lerrigo, Marion O. and Southard, Helen. Facts Aren't Enough. Chicago: American Medical Association, 1962.

Books for parents and children
(four to eight years old) to share

de Schweinitz, Karl. Growing Up. New York: The Macmillan Company, 1967. Fourth ed.

Frey, Marguerite Kurth. I Wonder, I Wonder. St. Louis: Concordia Publishing House, 1967.

Levine, Milton I. and Seligmann, Jean H. A Baby Is Born. New York: Golden Press, 1966.

May, Julian. Living Things and Their Young. Chicago: Follett Publishing Co., 1969.

Meeks, Esther K. and Bagwell, Elizabeth. The World of Living Things. Chicago: Follett Publishing Co., 1969.

Meilach, Dona Z. and Mandel, Elias. A Doctor Talks to 5-to-8-Year-Olds. Chicago: Budlong Press, 1967.

Books for children five to eight years old

Blough, G. O. Animals and Their Young. New York: Harper & Row, 1958.

de Santis, Mallen. Bubble Baths and Hair Bows. Garden City, N.Y.: Doubleday & Co., 1963.

Justus, May. New Boy in School. New York: Hastings House, 1963.

Kelling, Furn. This Is My Family. Nashville, Tenn.: Broadman Press, 1963.

Krasilovsky, Phyllis. The Very Little Boy. Garden City, N.Y.: Doubleday & Co., 1962.

———. The Very Little Girl. Garden City, N.Y.: Doubleday & Co., 1953.

Mattmuller, Felix. We Want a Little Sister. Minneapolis: Lerner Publication Co., 1965.

Meeks, Esther K., and Bagwell, Elizabeth. Families Live Together. Chicago: Follett Publishing Co., 1969.

———. How New Life Begins. Chicago: Follett Publishing Co., 1969.

Selsam, Millicent E. Egg to Chick. New York: International Publishers, 1946.

———. Plenty of Fish. New York: Harper & Row, 1960.

———. Terry and the Caterpillars. New York: Harper & Row, 1962.

Films for children five to eight years old

Beginning Responsibility: Doing Things for Ourselves in School, 1963. Coronet Films.

How Does a Garden Grow? 1962. Film Associates.

Human and Animal Beginnings, 1965. E. C. Brown Trust, University of Oregon.

Kittens: Birth and Growth, 1958. Bailey Films.

Living and Growing, 1957. Churchill Films.

Mother Hen's Family: The Wonder of Birth, 1953. Coronet Films.

Tad, the Frog, 1965. Coronet Films.

Poster pictures for children five to seven years old

Fricke, Irma B. Beginning the Human Story: A New Baby in the Family (with teacher's guide). Chicago: Scott, Foresman & Co., 1967.

Transparencies for children five to eight years old

Characteristics of Boys and Girls, 20 visuals, color, 1967. 3M Company.

The Family, 20 visuals, color, 1967. 3M Company.

Family Health, 20 visuals, color, 1967. 3M Company.

Living Things from Living Things, 20 visuals, color, 1967. 3M Company.

Books for parents and children (nine to twelve years old) to share

de Schweinitz, Karl. Growing Up. New York: The Macmillan Company, 1967. Fourth ed.

Hummel, Ruth. **Wonderfully Made.** St. Louis: Concordia Publishing House, 1967.

Levine, Milton I. and Seligmann, Jean H. **Human Reproduction.** New York: Harper & Row, 1967.

May, Julian. **How We Are Born.** Chicago: Follett Publishing Co., 1969.

————. **Man and Woman.** Chicago: Follett Publishing Co., 1969.

Books for children nine to twelve years old

Carson, Rachel. **The Sea Around Us.** New York: Golden Press, 1958.

————. **Under the Sea Wind.** New York: Oxford University Press, 1952.

Cosgrove, Margaret. **Eggs—and What Happens Inside Them.** New York: Dodd, Mead & Co., 1966.

Darling, Louis. **Chickens and How To Raise Them.** New York: William Morrow & Co., 1955.

Follett, Robert J. R. **Your Wonderful Body.** Chicago: Follett Publishing Co., 1961.

Lewis, Lucia. **The First Book of Microbes.** New York: Franklin Watts, 1955.

May, Julian. **Living Things and Their Young.** Chicago: Follett Publishing Co., 1969.

Parker, Bertha Morris. **The Stream of Life.** New York: Harper & Row, 1958.

Films for children nine to twelve years old

Animal Reproduction, 1966. Journal Films.

Human Growth, 1962. Wexler Film Productions.

Life in a Cell, 1956. Colburn Film Distributors.

Microbes and Their Control, 1963. Film Associates.

Salmon Story, 1950. Encyclopedia Britannica Films.

The Story of Menstruation, 1946. Walt Disney Studios, Kimberly-Clark Corporation.

Transparencies for children
nine to twelve years old

Body Changes at Puberty, 20 visuals, color, 1967. 3M
   Company.
Health and Happiness of the Family, 20 visuals, color,
   1967. 3M Company.
Heredity, 20 visuals, color, 1967. 3M Company.
How Life Begins, 20 visuals, color, 1967. 3M Company.
Range of Family Characteristics, 20 visuals, color, 1967.
   3M Company.
Science #3 Biology, pp. 63–64, "Amoeba," "Para-
   mecia." 3M Company.